COMPACT TIME

A SHORT HISTORY OF LIFE ON EARTH
COMPACT TIME

JOHN C. WALTON

Copyright © 2021 John C. Walton

The moral right of the author has been asserted.

Apart from any fair dealing for the purposes of research or private study, or criticism or review, as permitted under the Copyright, Designs and Patents Act 1988, this publication may only be reproduced, stored or transmitted, in any form or by any means, with the prior permission in writing of the publishers, or in the case of reprographic reproduction in accordance with the terms of licences issued by the Copyright Licensing Agency. Enquiries concerning reproduction outside those terms should be sent to the publishers.

Matador
9 Priory Business Park,
Wistow Road, Kibworth Beauchamp,
Leicestershire. LE8 0RX
Tel: 0116 279 2299
Email: books@troubador.co.uk
Web: www.troubador.co.uk/matador
Twitter: @matadorbooks

ISBN 978 1800461 246

British Library Cataloguing in Publication Data.
A catalogue record for this book is available from the British Library.

Printed and bound by CPI Group (UK) Ltd, Croydon, CR0 4YY
Typeset in 11pt Minion Pro by Troubador Publishing Ltd, Leicester, UK

Matador is an imprint of Troubador Publishing Ltd

When one has sought long for the clue to a secret of nature, and is rewarded by grasping some part of the answer, it comes as a blinding flash of revelation: it comes as something new, more simple and at the same time more aesthetically satisfying than anything one would have created in one's own mind. This conviction is of something revealed, and not something imagined.

W. Lawrence Bragg

I know that most men – not only those considered clever, but even those who are very clever, and capable of understanding most difficult scientific, mathematical, or philosophic problems – can very seldom discern even the simplest and most obvious truth if it be such as to oblige them to admit the falsity of conclusions they have formed, perhaps with much difficulty – conclusions of which they are proud, which they have taught to others, and on which they have built their lives.

Leo Tolstoy

Contents

List of Illustrations	ix
Acknowledgements	xi
Prologue: Recognising and Weighing Presuppositions	xiii

1: Conventional Earth Chronology — 1
- Time is a Mysterious Aspect of Reality — 1
- Geoscience Appropriates the Uniformitarian Straitjacket — 3
- The Ascendancy of Radiometric Dating Methods — 6
- Isochrons Rule the Dating Game — 14
- Fragility of Radiohalos and Fission Tracks — 21
- Conventional Age Determinations: The Default Mode — 23
- Confirmation Bias — 24

2: The Extraordinary Pervasiveness of Radiocarbon — 33
- The Radiocarbon Time Domain: A New Prospect — 33
- Radiocarbon Permeates the Whole Geologic Column — 39
- Radiocarbon and Dinosaurs — 44
- A Profound Challenge for Deep Time Chronology — 48

3: Downsizing Geologic Deep Time — 51
- Multitudes of Catastrophes — 51
- A Composite All-in-One Giga-Geologic Catastrophe? — 57

4: Footprints of the Giga-Catastrophe	**66**
Flood Narratives from Every Continent	66
When Did the Giga-Catastrophe Take Place?	72
5: A Carbon Clock for Compact Time	**78**
Large-Scale Burial of Carbon	79
Quantitative Model for ^{14}C Evolution after the Giga-Catastrophe	81
Historical Perspective on Radiocarbon Dating of Bronze Age Materials	85
Comparison of Conventional ^{14}C and CpT Model Dates with Archaeo-Historical Dates	90
Radiocarbon Dating and Dendrochronology: An Intimate Relationship	94
6: Dinosaur Remnants, Fossils and Compact Time	**103**
Soft Tissues in Dinosaur Fossils	103
Soft Spots in Rock Strata	111
Resolving Anomalies	116
1,500 Centuries of Stone Chipping?	117
7: Outcomes and Implications	**127**
Compact Time and the Geologic Column	127
Where are the Fossils of Modern Human Beings?	132
Precambrian Strata and the Age of the Earth	136
8: Compact Time and Ideology	**141**
Compact Time's Sound Base	141
The Vastness of Molecule Spaces	145
Design Eclipses Neo-Darwinian Evolution	148
Compact Time and Belief Systems	151
Index	159

LIST OF ILLUSTRATIONS

Chart:	Comparing Deep Time with Compact Time	xxii
Figure 1.1:	Uranium-238 and its Radioactive Decay Products	8
Figure 1.2:	The Geologic Timescale According to the ICS	12
Figure 1.3:	Typical Whole-Rock Isochron Plot	16
Figure 1.4:	Confirmation Bias	24
Figure 2.1:	Graphic Representation of the Isotopes of Carbon	34
Figure 2.2:	Radioactive Decay of Carbon-14.	35
Figure 2.3:	Principle of Radiocarbon Dating	36
Figure 2.4:	Coal Seams of the Permian Galilee Basin, Queensland	43
Figure 2.5:	Mounted Fossils of Two Species of Dinosaur	45
Figure 3.1:	Upper Cretaceous Turbidites from the Point Loma Formation, California	54
Figure 3.2:	Oviraptorosauria Skeletons	56
Figure 3.3:	Tōhoku Tsunami Aftermath, Sendai Airport	59
Figure 3.4:	Mount St. Helens Eruption Plume from the South	60
Figure 4.1:	Geographical Distribution of Flood Legends	70
Figure 4.2:	Common Elements in Two Hundred Flood Legends	71
Figure 4.3:	Age Spread of the World's Most Ancient Trees	74
Figure 4.4:	Bristlecone Pine, White Mountains, California	75
Figure 5.1:	Time Profile of the $^{14}C/C$ Ratio Before, During and After the Giga-Catastrophe	82

♦ ix

Figure 5.2:	Effect of the Giga-Catastrophe on Radiocarbon Dates – the CpT Model Ages	84
Figure 5.3:	Relationship Between Archaeo-Historical Ages and Calibrated ^{14}C Ages, Together with the CpT Model from Equation (2)	92
Figure 5.4:	The IntCal13 Calibration Curve for Radiocarbon Dates	96
Figure 5.5:	Cross Sections Through a 3,046-Year-Old Great Basin Bristlecone Pine	97
Figure 5.6:	Cross-Matching of a Tree-Ring Pattern with a Master Dendrochronology	98
Figure 6.1:	Soft Tissue Fragments from the Marrow Cavity of a T. Rex Femur	107
Figure 6.2:	Unmineralised Triceratops Brow Horn and Internal Soft Tissues	108
Figure 6.3:	Dr Brand with Miocene Baleen Whale Fossil	112
Figure 6.4:	Fossil Squid Ink Sac from Wiltshire, and Artist's Drawing of the Squid	113
Figure 6.5:	Diorama of Burgess Shale Sponges and Arthropods	115
Figure 7.1:	Radiocarbon-Derived Compact Time Chronology for Earth History	128
Figure 7.2:	Polystrate Fossil Trees	131
Chart 8.1:	Head-to-Head Comparison of World Chronologies	146
Figure 8.1:	Complex Structure of ATP Synthase Molecular Motor	148
Figure 8.2:	Coded Information in the Nucleotide Sequences of DNA	149

Acknowledgements

I'm deeply appreciative of the many who helped in the preparation of this book. I thank Dr Geoffrey Aori, whose thoughtful encouragement gave me the motivation to start writing it. I particularly thank Dr Duncan Bayliss, Dr Alastair Noble, Ms Emma J. S. Walton and Dr Andrew Snelling for critically reading the draft manuscript and for making many important suggestions for clarifying and improving it. Thanks too to Drs Mark Armitage, Leonard Brand, Ariel Roth, Tim Standish, Phil Wilby and the late Harold Coffin for generously donating high-quality photos from their personal collections. I also thank Faye Booth for so thoroughly and professionally editing the text. I'm very grateful to my wife, Jane, who has been hugely supportive throughout and who was immensely helpful in proofreading the text.

I'm also very appreciative of the proprietors of the periodical *Origins* and the Geoscience Research Institute, Loma Linda, California for publishing over many years so many interesting and thoughtful papers and articles pertaining to science and faith. They opened my understanding to the shaky foundations of evolutionary geoscience and to alternative views of world history. Dr Andrew Snelling's two-volume *Earth's Catastrophic*

Past is a work of massive scholarship and is a seminal achievement. The ideas developed in my book owe much to reports and evidence I first encountered in these publications.

Prologue

Recognising and Weighing Presuppositions

The theorems and results in mathematical physics are not theorems and results about Nature, but about our description of it.
Gerard 't Hooft

Truth, in science, can be defined as the working hypothesis best fitted to open the way to the next better one.
Konrad Lorenz

During the 18th and 19th centuries, the scientific method gathered such prestige that more and more subject disciplines adopted it to advance their causes. As science spread, it underwent notable changes to accommodate itself to the large dissimilarities in the various disciplines. The importance of laboratory experiments and testable predictions in support of theories and conclusions declined. Today, 'hard' sciences, backed by controlled experiments and mathematical formalism, are flanked by 'soft' sciences lacking methodological rigour. The difference is well understood by professional scientists but tends to be neglected or ignored by the general public and by the media. In soft sciences like evolutionary geology and biology, colourful and attention-grabbing narrative 'scenarios' hold prominent places. These are developed either by imaginative extrapolations from observational data or by 'plausible' deductions from central approved theories. To illustrate, Jerry Coyne, in his highly acclaimed book *Why Evolution is True*, offers the following story about the fossil fish *Tiktaalik* to explain the emergence of land creatures:

> *[Some Tiktaaliks] were bold enough to venture out of the water on their sturdy fin-limbs, perhaps to make their way to another stream… to avoid predators, or perhaps to find food among the many giant insects that had already evolved. If there were advantages to venturing onto land, natural selection could mould those explorers from fish into amphibians. That first small step ashore proved a great leap for vertebrate-kind, ultimately leading to every land-dwelling creature with a backbone.*[1]

It's a delightful yarn, but its speculative and imaginative character is immediately apparent, as is its dependence on the central theory of evolution. Were *Tiktaalik*'s fin-limbs really sturdy enough for walking? Could *Tiktaaliks* actually achieve anything out of water except flapping and gasping? Could *Tiktaaliks* digest the supposed giant insects? Would *Tiktaaliks* in fact be able to maintain breeding positions out of their natural element of water? Could fertilisation of fish egg by sperm occur on land so that vertebrate-kind could experience the great leap proposed? Would natural selection really be able to mould these fish into amphibians? Observational or laboratory study is not possible, so these and other questions like them remain unanswered. It is easy to imagine Baloo, in Kipling's *The Jungle Book*, telling virtually the same *Just So* story to Mowgli as he explains, "…and that's how the salamander got his four legs".

Clearly this kind of 'science' is far removed from experimentally tested physical science. Subtle presuppositions and assumptions underlie scenarios like these, often derived from ideology and unsupported by experiment. They certainly lack rigour and testability, yet too often they are accorded the same level of trustworthiness as hard science.

The scientific method seeks regular and repeatable laws and relationships to account for the working of nature. Singular, unique events like miracles are not susceptible to study by this means. Nor are spiritual experiences or inspirational insights. Science is not equipped to evaluate the validity or otherwise of these phenomena. However, scientists began to disregard or discount them.

Scientific laws and scenarios are human constructs that *model* reality. Some models are good, some poor, but all are only approximate. It's a grave mistake to regard them as claims of absolute truth or exact descriptions of reality. Scientific models always change and develop over time. That doesn't necessarily make earlier theories and models 'wrong', but rather, more elaborate and sophisticated models are developed. New ways of looking at things emerge, or more accurate equipment is designed, and the results change what is known. Nothing in science should be treated as fixed or immutable.

Regrettably, the distinction between model and reality became blurred in the public mind. The idea that a *complete* description of the universe could be obtained in terms of only natural laws and forces began to dominate as the cultural mindset. In science, naturalism gradually became the default philosophical option.

A key requirement of naturalism, though, is a scientific description of biological phenomena. Currently this is supplied by neo-Darwinian evolution. The word 'evolution' has several different meanings, ranging from just 'change over time' to full 'molecules-to-man' evolution. In this book, 'Darwinian evolution' or 'neo-Darwinian evolution' are used in the sense of total molecules-to-man progression, unless otherwise indicated. The mechanism by which neo-Darwinian evolution advances rests on natural selection working with random mutations. The complex working of population genetics, plus the randomness of mutations, means that, at a minimum, hundreds of millions of years are required to account for the richness and diversity of Earth's biological kingdoms. This Deep Time (DpT) has become an article of faith, ardently taught and vigorously defended in many branches of science.

Most of us grew up with Deep Time and instinctively view the geological and biological features of our world through lenses tinted with it. It needs to be recognised, however, that Deep Time was constructed by selecting only extremely slow-ticking clocks. Deep Time clocks were chosen with mechanisms that revolved to the snail's pace of hundreds of millions of years. Radiometric dating methods, of elements that decay with half-lives of this order, have been given the priority in the establishment of Deep Time chronology. Other chronometers were and are neglected, forgotten, or explained away.

My interest in Deep Time has been stimulated by hearing about rapid, high-energy environmental events and related circumstances that have come to light recently. For example, cataclysmic flooding of Lake Missoula is now thought to account for the vast geological changes in Eastern Washington and the Columbia Gorge. Geological carving of canyons and the deposition of layered strata are everywhere declared to take millions of years. In conflict with this, the eruption of Mount St. Helens demonstrated that such features can be obtained in only days. More and more turbidites, and related strata attributed to rapid underwater flows of sediment, are being recognised in the geologic column. Millions of polystrate, petrified trees, passing through multiple strata, have been found, particularly in coal measures.

One of the most startling discoveries, that's very challenging for Deep Time, is the finding of soft tissues in fossil dinosaur bones. Professor Mary Schweitzer's discoveries of stretchy protein, and even preserved blood vessels, in fossil *T. rex* bones were published in the top journal *Science*. She encountered a storm of hostility and disbelief from Deep Timers who were well aware of the impossibility of fleshy tissues surviving sixty-six million years. Her findings have, however, been fully confirmed and substantially extended. Other scientists have since made similar discoveries. When Dr Mark Armitage published his discovery of soft tissues in a triceratops horn, his academic colleagues were outraged and he was summarily dismissed from his post at California State University. He subsequently sued Cal State and was awarded a substantial sum in compensation. Chemistry is my profession, so I knew there is certainly no way soft protein-containing tissues can survive in fossils for sixty-six million years.

These discoveries started me wondering how soundly based Deep Time is. Is it backed by reliable experimentation, and does it have methodological rigour? Or are its sinews really presuppositions and assumptions derived from unproven theory? Has the well-known phenomenon of confirmation bias led to the unconscious selection of data 'acceptable' to naturalism and to the filtering out of discordant data? A thorough investigation of Deep Time and its foundations appeared to be due. Radiometric dating methods are the key tool employed in support of Deep Time. There are many of these methods, but radiocarbon dating stands out because its basis is different from most of the others'. To me this seemed a good place to start examining the evidence.

Radiocarbon (also called carbon-14) decays over a time range of only thousands of years, and the principle behind it is different from other radiometric clocks. It was eye-opening to discover that *undecayed* radiocarbon permeates the whole geologic column; it's even in fossil dinosaur bones! The presence of short-lived radiocarbon in fossils implies a compact timescale of only thousands of years for all the fossil-bearing strata. Radiocarbon dating leads to a chronology for earth history of the order of five to ten thousand years. I've christened this the Compact Time model (CpT). Numerous lines of evidence, including historical data from the Stone and Bronze Ages, plus geological and palaeontological discoveries, make sense in the light of this timetable. The implications of Compact Time for the geologic column and for human fossils are profound, as are the consequences for belief systems.

Questioning Deep Time is an unacceptable pursuit for individuals working in the evolutionary sciences. My background in chemical science is somewhat divorced from this. I've been engaged in academic research in organic chemistry for over thirty years. I've published hundreds of articles and several books, particularly on the properties of reactive free radicals. Timing the speed at which molecules undergo their reactions is very important in gaining an understanding of their behaviour. Many 'clocks' have been developed for doing this, including kinetic electron paramagnetic resonance (EPR) spectroscopy. In my research I've applied EPR spectroscopy, and many other timing methods, to the study of molecular transformations. When in 1993 the Royal Society of Chemistry awarded me a silver medal for some of my research, the citation mentioned this: "Distinguished for an outstanding contribution to our knowledge of the behaviour of reactive radicals and, in particular, the timing of the events in which they are involved." This background in molecular timing and dynamics has contributed to my long-term interest in timing devices and in chronology. I maintain, therefore, that I'm fittingly qualified to carry out an independent but well-informed evaluation of the basics of Deep Time.

Of course, every scientist has a personal belief system. This might be atheism, naturalism, agnosticism, deism, theism or other. Complete objectivity is a myth, and all these beliefs have a bearing on choices and how evidence is interpreted. I'm a practising Christian of a conservative persuasion, and am well aware of how this can colour my perceptions. I do contend, however, that my conclusions and interpretations are no more likely to be biased than those of naturalists. The outcome should be judged by the materials presented, and the rationale behind the conclusions drawn.

Long ages and timescales are hugely significant for belief systems; a lot is riding on them. For this reason alone, it is imperative to closely evaluate the evidence that underpins them. Deep Time is an inescapable requirement of neo-Darwinian evolution. Darwin wrote that his theory needs "numerous, successive slight modifications" for the development of each living species. The biosphere today contains many thousands of distinct life forms, such that a vast number of these successive slight modifications would be required. Each of these has to be favoured by natural selection, successfully passed to offspring and spread to the whole population. Accordingly, hundreds of millions (and probably billions) of years are required between the appearance of the first life form on Earth and the present day. Without Deep Time, neo-Darwinian evolution certainly fails.

The consequences for Bible-based faiths are equally significant. If Deep Time is the true chronology of life on Earth, then the creation accounts in Genesis are found to be unhistorical and misleading in numerous ways. For example, life would have originated long before the six or seven thousand years indicated. *Homo sapiens* emerged hundreds of thousands of years ago, so that all human beings could not be descended from one pair: Adam and Eve. Death did not originate in Eden, but had been an integral part of life's panorama for long ages. Deep Time necessitates a radical reinterpretation of origins not envisaged by either Old or New Testament writers.

Deep Time methods are less certain than most people have been led to believe. It became clear that radiometric dating methods have serious problems and that the results they give are contingent on the assumptions they rely on. This book brings together recent evidence that strongly suggests some of those assumptions need re-evaluating. Following through on this, and focusing attention on alternative, faster-running clocks, leads to quite different answers and to the short Compact Time timescale.

This book is written for ordinary people who are interested in how and when life came into existence on Earth. Deep Time underpins neo-Darwinian evolution, which is proclaimed by naturalists to be as well established as the heliocentric solar system. This book directly controverts this and is written to encourage questioning of authoritarian assertions like this from 'soft' science sources.

John C. Walton
St. Andrews, UK

Endnotes

1   Jerry A. Coyne, *Why Evolution is True*, Oxford University Press, Oxford, 2009, p. 41.

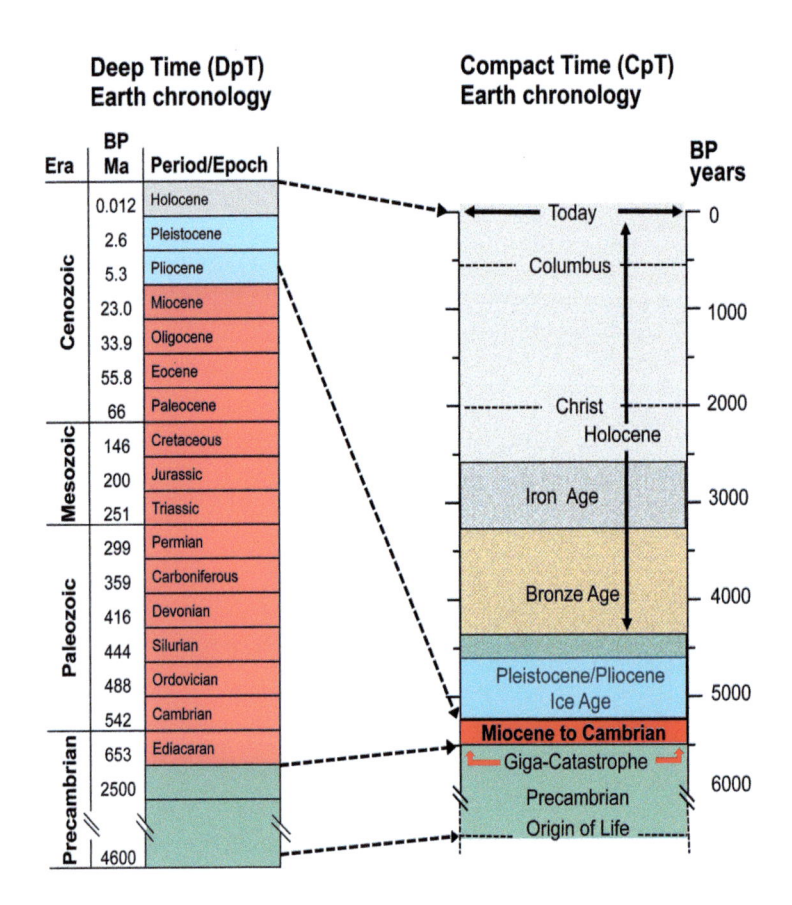

Chart: *Comparing Deep Time with Compact Time.*

Chapter 1

Conventional Earth Chronology

The human understanding when it has once adopted an opinion… draws all things else to support and agree with it. And though there be a greater number and weight of instances to be found on the other side, yet these it either neglects or despises, or else by some distinction sets aside or rejects.
Francis Bacon, *Novum Organum*

Confirmation bias is the tendency to search for, interpret, favor, and recall information in a way that affirms one's prior beliefs or hypotheses.
Scott Plous, *The Psychology of Judgment and Decision Making*

Time is a Mysterious Aspect of Reality

Time is the factor that marks off the constant progress of our existence. It presents us with a continuous succession of events from the past, through the present, to the future. We take this passage of time for granted but it remains mysterious. It's a uniquely valuable commodity for us, but it can't be banked, and it can't be stored! It's one of the most difficult aspects of our universe to understand. There is no agreed definition of exactly what time is. Why does it move in only one direction? Sometimes we would like to dismount from its headlong rush, but we can't avoid the present and we can't prevent the future from arriving! Understandably, we would love to know how far into the past the stream of events extended and if it will continue indefinitely into the future!

We derive a good deal of quiet amusement from speculating about how old people are and checking the vintage of their possessions. It's the kind of mind game most people enjoy! It's the basis of several popular TV shows. But it can have a serious purpose too. The ability to correctly assess age is useful because age has a bearing on the value of things, on their durability, on where they were made and sometimes on who made them. Curiosity about age extends beyond the people, furniture and houses in our orbit to larger things such as monuments and cities. At another level, the ages of environmental features such as forests, rivers and hills also draw our attention. Not surprisingly, ideas about how old planet Earth itself is have been around virtually since the start of recorded history.

The passing of time can be observed and measured. As time goes by, the material fabric of our environment, and of ourselves, gradually degrades. We notice these downhill changes and, from determining their extent, we can develop means of measuring the passage of time. This degradation is enshrined in the second law of thermodynamics. Technically this law refers to the constant increase in entropy in isolated systems. On planet Earth this is revealed in ever-increasing disorder. Energy always goes towards less available forms. Strangely, this increase in entropy is the only aspect of reality that calls for time to move only in the forward direction. Physicist Arthur Eddington, in his book *The Nature of the Physical World*, dubbed this the "arrow of time".[1]

The first appearance of living things, and particularly when human beings originated, appears strongly coupled to the age of the Earth. From place to place, the Earth displays extreme variations in appearance and composition. Furthermore, the rates of dynamic natural processes range from almost infinitesimally slow to extremely rapid, and many are cyclical so, over time, ideas about the age of the Earth have covered huge ranges of years. Chronology is the crucial backbone of history, and so the age of the Earth and of its physical features are vital factors in developing valid historical and geological perspectives. However, it can't be too strongly emphasised that the cultural, philosophical and religious convictions of the historians, scientists and theologians who have tackled the chronology of Earth have hugely influenced their conclusions.

Geoscience Appropriates the Uniformitarian Straitjacket

The Scottish geologist and physician James Hutton, working in the 18th century, became convinced that the history of Earth could be explained by understanding how processes such as erosion and sedimentation work slowly in the present day. He was influential in popularising what came to be called uniformitarianism: the system of explaining Earth's geological features in terms of presently observable natural processes.[2] Uniformitarianism was enthusiastically embraced by earth scientists in the 19th century. The global catastrophe(s) previously invoked to explain crustal features were essentially unpredictable and unquantifiable; consequently, geoscience was confined to the role of being merely descriptive. The rates and mechanisms of present-day processes, in contrast, could be studied and quantified first-hand, enabling numerical models to be constructed. Uniformitarianism paved the way for these quantitative models to be extrapolated into the past. Geoscientists could then apply dynamic timing models and statistical tools to past geological processes, and so build up seemingly more scientifically rigorous descriptions of geological phenomena. Uniformitarianism therefore materially enhanced the status of geoscience and enabled it to claim some of the lustre and prestige associated with mathematically underpinned disciplines like physics and chemistry.

William Smith, a land surveyor working in the 18th and early 19th centuries, devoted most of his life to studying geological strata in England. He carefully observed, documented and evaluated the types of fossils they contained. He made the momentous discovery that sedimentary strata could be characterised by the fossil suites they contained, and that these usually succeeded one another *in the same order*. Over the next half-century or so, heroic work based on this principle was carried forward by him and pioneering luminaries of earth science such as Sir Roderick Murchison, Sir Charles Lyell and Adam Sedgwick. Together with botanists such as Adolphe-Théodore Brongniart in France, and other professionals in Germany, they slowly pieced together a complete diagram of the worldwide succession of strata arranged in relative chronological order.

The geologic column they developed for strata around the world (illustrated in the Reference Chart on page 12 and in Figure 1.2) was divided into four main eras, each subdivided into periods. The latter were given picturesque names, such as the Jurassic period after the Jura Mountains, and the Cretaceous period from the Latin word '*creta*' for chalk. The column was a magnificent achievement, and vividly illustrates the relative timing of the deposition of individual strata. It was safe to conclude that the lower a stratum was in this column, the older it was. Speculation about the 'absolute' dating of the strata in 'years before the present' (BP, YbP) had, of course, been going on long before the sequence was completely mapped.

The combined thickness of the sedimentary strata was very great. The three eras from the top of the Cenozoic to the bottom of the Palaeozoic have a maximum thickness of more than ten thousand metres of sediment! Uniformitarian thinking supposed these sediments had, for the most part, accumulated at the same rate as modern depositional processes. This gave rise to the view that many *millions* of years must have been involved in the deposition of the column. Lyell's multi-volume work *Principles of Geology* set out his concept that these features were shaped by presently observable processes acting over immensely long periods of time.[3] His work advocated a vast age for the Earth, and powerfully influenced future naturalists, geologists and biologists.

Efforts were made during the 19th century to construct absolute timing methods, termed 'geological hourglasses', based on sediment deposition or denudation rates of selected processes. It proved to be impossible to achieve anything dependable, because deposition and erosion rates varied so much with local factors such as alterations in the supply of sediment, the subsidence of the floor of the basin in which the sediments were accumulating, or alternating periods of scour and fill.

A famous method originally worked out in the 1890s by John Joly, Professor of Geology at the University of Dublin, calculated the age of the sea as eighty to one hundred million years (Ma) from the accumulation of sodium (salt) in the oceans. Initially, this proved to be a popular result and was widely circulated. Gradually the opinion gained ground, influenced by, amongst other things, considerations from evolutionary biology, that the Earth must be much older than this. Deep Time chronology (DpT) was becoming the norm amongst academic scientists.

The Ascendancy of Radiometric Dating Methods

Geochronology took on a completely new aspect in the early 20th century. Arthur Holmes, from Northumbria in England, was the central figure in this transformation. After studying physics and geology at Imperial College, Holmes went on an expedition to Mozambique and then had a spell in oil exploration in Burma. In 1925 he became Professor of Geology at Durham University, and much of his research work on radiometric methods of dating took place during his time in Durham. He transferred to Edinburgh University in 1943, and his major books were published during his tenure there. He had exceptional talent for writing in clear and coherent prose. His books, such as *Principles of Physical Geology*, contain superb illustrations and engaging quotations. They ran through multiple editions and became classics of earth science.

Holmes was an enthusiastic advocate of Deep Time. He revealed his mindset early on, in the introduction to his popular book *The Age of the Earth*, through his disparagement of Hebrew chronology as found in the Pentateuch; followed by the admiration he voiced for the long ages of Aryan mythology with the particulars he adapted so charmingly from the Rig Vedas. Holmes brought together a great deal of evidence that the sea/salt and other sedimentary hourglasses were hopelessly unreliable. He noted that the accumulation of salt in the sea would require the rocks to lose more sodium than they could ever have contained. He described the unknowably greater river flow rates in times of flood. He waxed almost lyrical in describing the huge and varied geological changes that had occurred, including:

The rise and fall of landforms, the invasion and retreat of seas, the growth of deltas and coral reefs, the eruptions of long extinct volcanoes, the swing of climate between tropical and glacial.[4]

Other huge events transforming the geological landscape included mountain building, vast surface flows of heated lava, and immense intrusions into rock formations of gigantic granite batholiths, some of these hundreds of miles in extent. All these events would have affected the composition and distribution of igneous and sedimentary rocks and caused wide variations in rates of erosion and deposition. Holmes rightly concluded that dates derived from depositional or erosional hourglasses would be hopelessly untrustworthy. He was looking for a chronological method that would avoid these problems.

In the 1890s in Paris, Marie Curie and her husband Pierre were processing, without any protective clothing, tons of the uranium minerals pitchblende and torbernite. This hazardous but brilliant research earned Marie undying fame for her discoveries of radioactivity and of the elements radium and polonium, but it also contributed to her untimely death from radiation-induced aplastic anaemia. The uranium and thorium in the minerals slowly converted by radioactive decay into lead and helium (see Figure 1.1).

Holmes was fascinated by this phenomenon, and soon recognised that the constancy of the decay rate and its imperviousness to essentially all environmental influences made it very promising as a means for dating minerals. If the amounts of uranium and its decay products in rocks and ores could be measured, then dates for their formation could be derived from its known rate of decay.

Means of making such measurements soon came to hand, as mass spectrometry was also discovered early in the 20th century. Progress was delayed by the First World War, but Francis Aston, at Cambridge University, built the first functioning mass spectrometer soon after the war ended. Procedures and instruments were refined during the 1920s and '30s, thus supplying the very technique Holmes needed to determine the amounts of individual uranium and lead isotopes in rock samples.

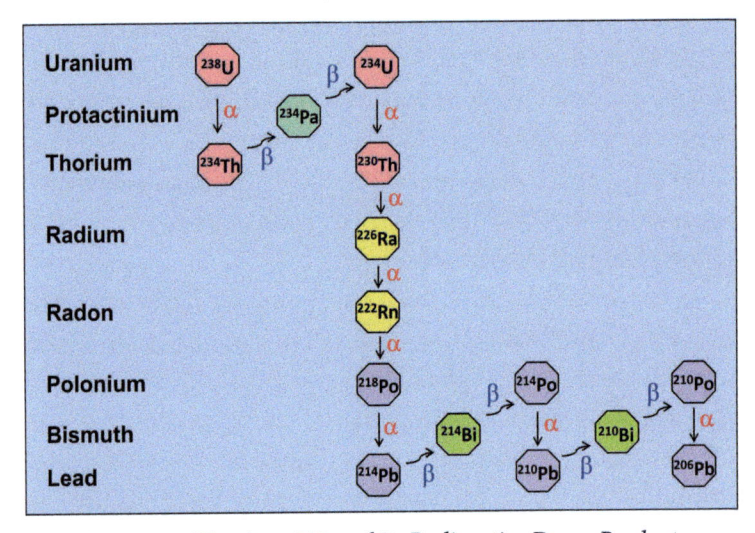

Figure 1.1: *Uranium-238 and its Radioactive Decay Products.*

Accurate means of quantifying helium in rock samples also became available, so W. D. Urry, at the Massachusetts Institute of Technology, succeeded in measuring the helium, radium and thorium content mainly of basalts, and thereby deriving ages for most of the periods in the geologic column. Helium is, however, a light gas, and easily escapes from rock and mineral matrices. Only rock samples that were considered to be retentive of helium could be dated this way. Deciding which samples were sufficiently fine-grained, fresh and otherwise suitable was a very subjective exercise. Scepticism of the ages of basalts obtained by this method was understandable.

Holmes, and the international group of scientists he worked

with, focused attention on the lead isotopes found in uranium minerals and lead ores. From measurements of uranium, thorium and lead in the minerals uraninite, pitchblende, thorite and others from localities all over the world, they derived ages ranging up to over 400 Ma BP for rocks from the Tertiary through to the Cambrian. The method was then applied to Precambrian ores and minerals from Europe, Australia and Canada, affording dates from 600–1,750 Ma BP.

The method was based on some important assumptions. First, that the initial amount of lead in the mineral, when it was first deposited, was known or could be derived from related data. Second, that the mineral had existed as part of a geologically closed system. It was essential that uranium, thorium or actinium, as well as their decay products, had not been added or removed during the time interval. Holmes made educated guesses about the initial amounts of lead from studying the lead composition of non-radiogenic rocks, and also by extrapolating from minerals with different extents of decay.

Rocks have experienced a huge range of environmental, ecological and tectonic assaults over geological time. These include storms, hurricanes, glacial episodes, climate swings from tropical to glacial, tsunamis, floods, sea-level changes, mountain building, volcanism, lava flows and immense plutonic intrusions. These transformations often occurred on much greater scales than are seen in the present day. Having cited these factors as reasons for rejecting the sea/salt and other depositional chronometers, Holmes was well aware of the bearing they had on radiometric methods. In relation to the assumption of closed systems, he conceded that "for a large number of the minerals that have been analysed this assumption cannot be granted".[5] Further: "The importance of this condition is emphasized by the fact that the lead method cannot, as yet, be applied to igneous rocks with any hope of success."[6]

Having admitted this much, Holmes nevertheless tried to

develop criteria to guide in the selection of mineral samples. He advocated two highly subjective criteria: "a scrutiny of the chemical composition" and the "physical state" of the mineral; that is, its 'freshness', grain size, colour etc. He also began the practice for a given rock sample of first assessing the period to which it belonged in the geologic column. If the chemical composition yielded a date at odds with this, then he believed it could safely be discounted. It is obvious that this leaves an open door for unconscious confirmation bias to sway the sample selection process. Holmes was honest enough to write, "In attempting to build up a time-scale based on lead-ratios it is clear that we have to steer a difficult course through a maze of data of very variable quality."[7] Such open-mindedness is notably lacking amongst Deep Time devotees today.

In their rock hosts, the parent and daughter radioactive elements continually experience the effects of percolating groundwaters. The environmental episodes referred to above will necessarily impact groundwater composition. A given episode may alter its acidity, ionic strength, temperature, flow rate, pressure, and the mix of dissolved minerals. Radioactive elements' solubilities will be affected. Additional radioactive materials from nearby sources might be deposited. Another common process is upward movement through the crust of hot magma originating deep in the Earth's mantle. Melting of the surrounding rock occurs, facilitating exchange of material. Mixing processes will also be augmented by the underground flow of heated hydrothermal fluids and gases. This indisputably results in exchange of elements along the fluid path by deposition and dissolution.

Supposing the rock host experiences one environmental episode per year of the type referred to above. Then in one million years, the rock will have been subject to a million such ecological assaults with their fluctuating effects from groundwater, hydrothermal fluids etc. For radiometric dating it must be assumed that the radioactive elements in a 100-Ma-old sample survived unchanged in a closed cocoon during one hundred million such environmental convulsions! A 1,000-Ma-old sample would have to retain its pristine condition through a *billion* environmental assaults! The likelihood that *any* rock matrix could remain closed during this number of ecological assaults seems incredibly remote. Yet this is the unavoidable assumption upon which much Deep Time chronology is based! A prudent person is fully entitled to remain sceptical of the validity of such an assumption and dubious of the resulting long-age data.

The mineral composition and the elemental isotope ratios in a rock sample that had actually passed through such an incredibly vast number of environmental transformations would bear little relation to the composition at the original time of deposition hundreds of millions of years previously. Of course, the quantities of parent and daughter elements in any sample today can easily be determined by the usual analytical techniques. But the simple radioactive decay law would not be applicable to them. Their relationship to the parent radioactive element would depend on a vast number of periods of dissolution and accumulation, all of unknown duration. Some complex average would result unrelated to total elapsed time. The only constant in the process would be the half-life of the radioactive decay, and this might figure as a minor component of the unknowably complex function relating parent to daughter.

Holmes had proposed the earliest geological timescale in the 1930s. He remained the leading figure in the field, updating this timescale from time to time as new results appeared. It is noteworthy, however, that by the 1950s Holmes' timescale had reached a form not much different from that accepted today. This timescale, as published in the second edition of his celebrated *Principles of Physical Geology*,[8] is compared in Figure 1.2 with the modern conventional geological timescale. The definitive version of this is maintained by the International Commission on Stratigraphy (ICS), which is part of the International Union of Geological Sciences.[9] Figure 1.2 was adapted from the most recent version of this.

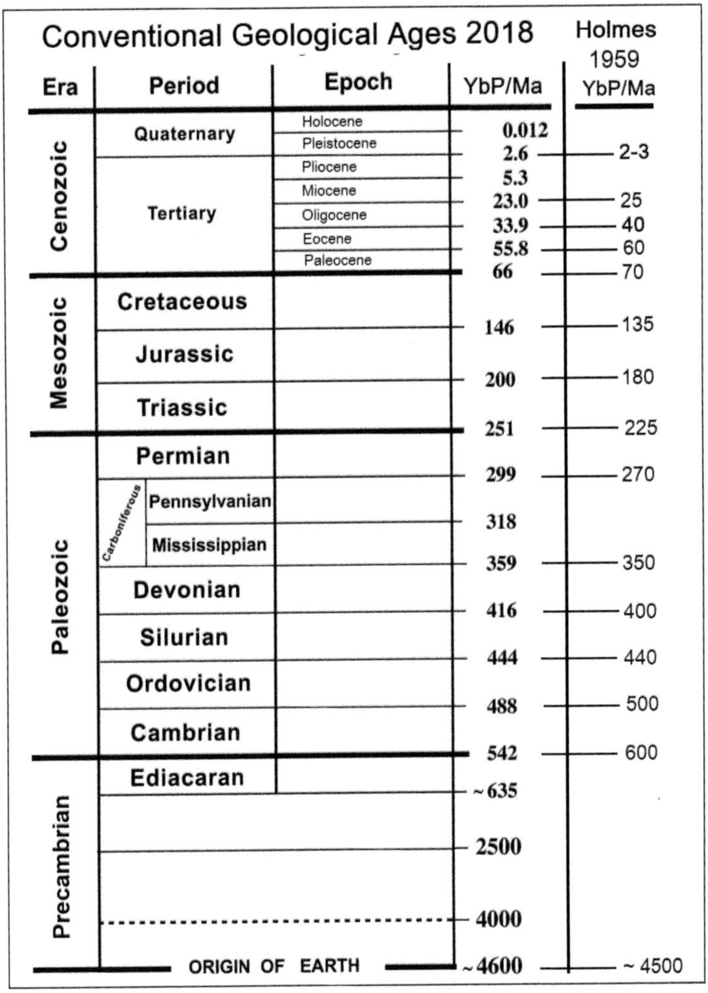

Era	Period	Epoch	YbP/Ma	Holmes 1959 YbP/Ma
Cenozoic	Quaternary	Holocene	0.012	
		Pleistocene	2.6	2-3
	Tertiary	Pliocene	5.3	
		Miocene	23.0	25
		Oligocene	33.9	40
		Eocene	55.8	60
		Paleocene	66	70
Mesozoic	Cretaceous		146	135
	Jurassic		200	180
	Triassic		251	225
Paleozoic	Permian		299	270
	Carboniferous Pennsylvanian		318	
	Mississippian		359	350
	Devonian		416	400
	Silurian		444	440
	Ordovician		488	500
	Cambrian		542	600
Precambrian	Ediacaran		~635	
			2500	
			4000	
	ORIGIN OF EARTH		~4600	~4500

Figure 1.2: *The Geologic Timescale According to the ICS. On the right is Arthur Holmes' timescale, published in 1959.*

The divisions of the geologic column are on the left and their conventional modern dates, in years before the present (BP), are in the fourth column. Considering that the construction dates of the two timescales differ by nearly sixty tumultuous years, their similarity is remarkable. The total time spans to the bottom of the Precambrian, representing the age of the Earth, in Holmes' and the modern version are practically identical. The time spans of the fossil-bearing sedimentary layers to the bottom of the Cambrian are almost unchanged. Adjustments to the boundaries of some of the other periods have been made, but the overall resemblance is very striking.

Biological science also underwent radical changes during the 19th century. Notions about the relatedness of living species were voiced even in the 18th century by Buffon, Diderot, Erasmus Darwin and others. Lamarck's publication in 1809 of his volume *Philosophie Zoologique* gave wide publicity to his theory of the inheritance of acquired characteristics. During the early and mid 19th century, intense debate took place about whether or not living things had evolved. Having read about the "struggle for existence" in T. R. Malthus's writings, Charles Darwin developed the concept of natural selection as the driving force of evolution. Alfred Russel Wallace had come to similar conclusions. The publication of Darwin's famous book *On the Origin of Species* in 1859 was seminal in directing future historical biology. Thomas H. Huxley powerfully campaigned for Darwin's theory which, before the start of the 20th century, had become the mainstream scientific explanation for the origin of all living species.

For the huge variety of living forms to originate by natural selection, immense periods of time would be required. The development of new organs and body plans could only take place gradually over many generations and through many intermediate forms. The spread of these changes through whole populations in the plant and animal kingdoms across the globe implied enormously lengthy ages. As might be expected, the colossal time span allotted to the Earth's geologic history by Holmes and his contemporary geochronologists resonated well with these developing evolutionary ideas in biology and palaeontology. Deep Time soon formed an essential component of both earth and biological sciences. During the 20th century it became deeply entrenched in the psyche of scientists working in these disciplines. In academic circles, questioning Deep Time became unthinkable and unacceptable.

Isochrons Rule the Dating Game

Of course, radiometric dating has advanced enormously since Holmes' day. New analytical techniques have been discovered, instrumentation has become far more sophisticated, and advances have been made in sample gathering and preparation. Many commercial and university laboratories around the world are now engaged in sample dating. The range of naturally occurring radioactive isotopes used in geochronology has also greatly expanded. Dozens of different elements are in use, but the most popular are the potassium-argon (K-Ar), rubidium-strontium (Rb-Sr), samarium-neodymium (Sm-Nd) and uranium-thorium-lead (U-Th-Pb) methods. A novel technique, the isochron method, was also invented, with potential to overcome some of the problems associated with single-rock 'model' ages. The expected advantage of the isochron method was that it would enable the amounts of any initial daughter element present in rock and mineral samples before the start of radioactive decay to be quantified.[10] Most modern radiometric dates are obtained by this isochron method.

Daughter elements in rocks exist as mixtures of several different isotopes (variant forms) with different mass numbers (atomic weights). One of these isotopes, one that is not part of the radioactive decay process, called a sister isotope, is chosen as a standard calibration marker. For example, rubidium with mass number 87 (^{87}Rb) decays to strontium with mass number 87 (^{87}Sr), but minerals also contain the sister isotope strontium-86 (^{86}Sr) that is not the end product of any decay process.

Similarly, samarium-147 decays to neodymium-143, but stable sister isotope neodymium-144 is also present in minerals and serves as the calibration marker in Sm-Nd radiometric dating. The chemical properties of the two sister isotopes are virtually identical, so very similar behaviour is expected in rock matrices. The amount of a sister isotope should remain constant over time so they can act as unchanging standards present in minerals and serve as the calibration marker in Sm-Nd radiometric dating.

To obtain an isochron age, a set of several samples will be collected from the same rock unit. When the set is of different minerals present in the same rock unit, they yield a 'mineral isochron age'. The distribution of the parent and daughter radioactive elements in the rock unit will usually be uneven. Alternatively, therefore, samples of the whole rock, without any separation of minerals, may be selected. A 'whole-rock isochron age', ideally the same as the mineral isochron age, is then obtained. A key assumption needed for the method to work is that the initial ratio, before decay, of the two sister isotopes (for example [^{87}Sr]/[^{86}Sr]) must be the same in all the samples. Individual samples will be analysed for the parent, daughter and sister elements, for example ^{87}Rb, ^{87}Sr and ^{86}Sr. The isochron then consists of a plot of the [^{87}Sr]/[^{86}Sr] ratio on the vertical y-axis against the [^{87}Rb]/[^{86}Sr] ratio on the horizontal x-axis (see Figure 1.3).

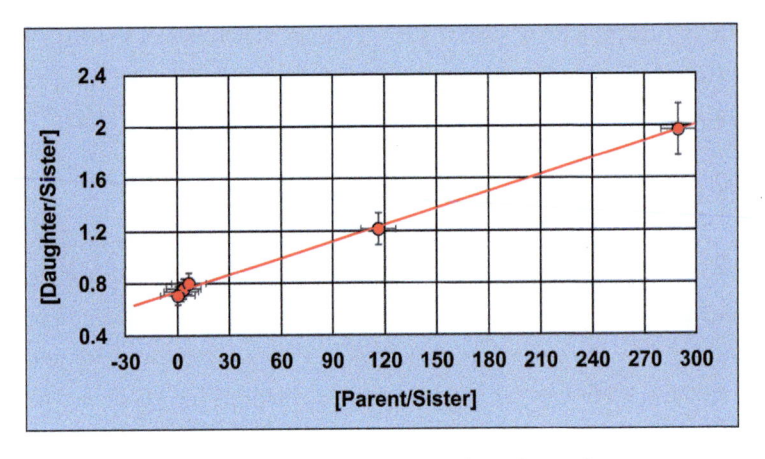

Figure 1.3: *Typical Whole-Rock Isochron Plot.*

The gradient of this graph yields the age of the rock, with luck independent of any daughter ^{87}Sr initially present. What is more, the amount of ^{87}Sr initially present can itself be estimated from the intercept on the y-axis. If the analytical data points show serious scatter, this is evidence of open-system behaviour and the resulting age may be discounted or 'reinterpreted'.

The isochron method has become the standard radiometric method for dating igneous rock and mineral samples. Many thousands of isochron ages have been published. All is not, however, as straightforward as the bare maths behind the isochron theory suggest. It is always good practice to test a novel scientific method with a problem whose outcome is already known. The reliability of the method can then be assessed depending on whether the result it generates agrees with that already established. Radiometric dating methods, including the isochron method, have been tested by applying them to rocks of known age. The New Zealand volcano Mount Ngauruhoe produced lava flows in 1949, 1954 and 1975. The Uinkaret Plateau in the Grand Canyon contains recent lava flows known to be less than one million years old. Samples from both sites were dated by the conventional K-Ar method involving individual rocks (model ages), and by several isochron methods based on different elements.[11-15]

Disturbingly, model ages obtained by the K-Ar method from several samples from the same rock, cover wide age spreads: some as much as millions of years. Astonishingly, as Table 1.1 reveals, the isochron methods yielded ages of hundreds of millions of years for recently formed rocks. Moreover, the isochrons obtained with different elements sharply disagreed with one another. The Pb-Pb isochron yielded the incredible age of nearly four billion years! The most troubling outcome was that for each set of samples the isochrons were good, straight lines, giving no evidence of open-system behaviour! The isochron method fared very badly in this crucial test and in others like it. If the method fails for rocks of known age, why should it be trusted for specimens of unknown age?

Rock Unit	Historic Age	Model K-Ar (Ma BP)	Isochron Ages (Ma BP) Rb-Sr	Sm-Nd	Pb-Pb
Mt. Ngauruhoe	[1949-75][a]	<0.27-3.5	133±87	197±160	3,908±390
Uinkaret Plateau	<1.2	1.2-20.7	1,143±220	916±570	2600

[a] Known dates AD of lava flows.

Table 1.1: *Isochron Ages (Ma BP) for Recent Rock Samples.*[14,16]

It's remarkable that straight-line plots are obtained at all from experimentally measured isotope ratios on sets of samples removed from natural rock units. Scatter is the norm for experimental data, particularly if the samples turn out to be anomalous or inconsistent! The obtention of good linear relationships raised the question of whether the isochron gradients reflect some other regular property of rock systems, rather than the time elapsed since their deposition!

Discordant isochrons are by no means isolated occurrences. Careful geologic fieldwork, coupled to isochron age determinations, has been carried out over many years by earth scientists. Their published research with popular isochron methods has been reviewed in detail by Andrew Snelling.[17] The Rb-Sr method is probably the most widely used for rock and mineral dating. Various geological situations were found where good linear Rb-Sr isochrons were obtained, yet these were anomalous, had no geological meaning and gave unacceptable age data.[18] It is now recognised that the key assumption of initially equal sister element [^{87}Sr]/[^{86}Sr] ratios for sample sets from within the same rock unit is often invalid.[19] Furthermore, suites of samples of different ages and different initial sister element ratios [^{87}Sr]/[^{86}Sr] still yielded linear isochrons![20]

Igneous rock suites are often contaminated by hot magma rising from the mantle deep below the Earth's crust. The [^{87}Rb]/[^{86}Sr] and [^{87}Sr]/[^{86}Sr] ratios were frequently found to correlate with one another in this situation, such that good linear plots were obtained, although the 'ages' bore no relation to the actual age of the rock. These plots were termed 'mantle isochrons' or 'pseudo-isochrons'. Magma mixing is recognised as a major process in the generation of igneous rocks. The measured Rb-Sr data, in these circumstances, will yield only an apparent isochron that is actually a mixing isochron. Of course, pseudo-isochrons are distinguished from true isochrons when the resultant 'age' disagrees with the conventional Deep Time age derived from the geologic column.

Another disquieting factor is the ease and rapidity with which Rb and Sr can be leached from fresh rocks. Leaching is also selective for one or other of the elements depending on the nature of the leaching fluid. Commonly, this results in a large loss of Sr and an increase in Rb, leading to a spread in Rb/Sr whole-rock ratios. These alterations due to atmospheric weathering and moving groundwater are systematic and regular, such that pseudo-isochrons, indistinguishable from true ones, are generated. The mounting evidence of mantle inheritance, open-system behaviour and the proliferation of false and anomalous isochrons attest to the unreliability of the Rb-Sr isochron method, and have led to a loss in its popularity.[18, 21]

The problems mentioned above also apply to isochron methods based on other elements. Potassium-argon isochrons suffer from additional problems because of the gaseous nature of the argon produced. Excess argon from the mantle is often incorporated in the rock units, whereas other rocks suffer from argon loss due to it diffusing out during heating. There is no way of determining definitively if either of these processes has occurred, so the resulting ages are doubtful. The atoms of uranium, thorium and lead are all mobile in rocks, which undermines whole-rock dating by this method. Lead migration within individual mineral grains and loss from them are so prevalent that interpreting the isotope data is largely down to the predisposition of the investigator.

The samarium-neodymium method has enjoyed a high reputation because Sm and Nd were thought to be less mobile. However, the method has other problems in that, because of the long half-life of Sm (106 billion years, Ga), it is difficult to find minerals with the reasonable spread of Sm/Nd ratios needed for isochron charts. Most age determinations have been restricted to garnets. Furthermore, unreliable initial $^{143}Nd/^{144}Nd$ ratios result, because long extrapolations of the isochrons are required. There is also evidence that Sm and Nd are not as immobile as claimed.

It is rarely possible to date a rock unit by all four of the popular isochron methods. Snelling describes a very illuminating study of four different rock units from the Grand Canyon, to which all four isochron methods were applied.[22] For every rock unit, all four methods gave discordant isochron ages. As Table 1.2 demonstrates, the results revealed some surprising systematic trends.

First, it was found that parent elements decaying by alpha-emission gave older ages than those decaying by beta-emission. Second, there was also a trend towards older ages from methods based on longer half-life elements. These trends hint that yet unknown factors other than elapsed time underlie the development of parent/daughter radio-element concentration ratios in rock systems. Statements commonly found in popular textbooks to the effect that different radiometric dating methods applied to the same rock are 'always in agreement' must be treated as absurd wishful thinking.

Method	Potassium-Argon	Rubidium-Strontium	Samarium-Neodymium	Uranium-Lead
Parent-daughter symbols	K-Ar	Rb-Sr	Sm-Nd	U-Pb
Half-life of parent (Ga)	1.25	49.2	106	4.47
Important applications	Human evolution timescale	Terrestrial and lunar rocks; meteorites	Terrestrial rocks; garnets	Geologic column boundaries
Principal problems	Contamination by old Ar; loss of Ar gas; mobility of K; open systems	Magma mixing; leaching of Rb and Sr; open systems	Long half-life; extrapolations; open systems	Mobility of Pb; discordant results; open systems
Outcomes & consequences	False isochrons; dates too old	False isochrons; dates meaningless	Unreliable isochrons; dates too old	Dates too old or meaningless

Table 1.2: *Summary of Popular Radiometric Dating Methods.*

Fragility of Radiohalos and Fission Tracks

The decay of radioactive elements can sometimes leave persistent, microscopic yet visible damage to crystal hosts. Uranium and thorium atoms tend to cluster within crystals of the mineral zircon. The radioactive nuclei emit alpha particles with considerable energies which depend on the particular emission process. The alpha particles spread out randomly in all directions and escape from minute zircon crystals into surrounding biotite material. They lose their energy to the biotite, most of it at the end of their trajectories. All the alpha particles with the same initial energy stop at the same distance from the centre, such that a sphere of discolouration develops in the crystal. On sectioning the biotite, the damage appears as a set of dark rings known as radiohalos (also known as pleochroic halos), each corresponding to a particular alpha decay process. Radiohalos can only form in solid crystalline structures. They are fragile and easily fade when heated, usually to only about 150°C. Radiohalos are abundant in granitic rocks from all periods of the geologic column, and in biotite-containing metamorphic rocks from many geologic periods.

Polonium isotopes are amongst the products of decay of uranium (see Figure 1.1). Polonium radiohalos have been observed in biotite sheets contained in granitic rocks from all periods of the geologic column. Usually these are close (within millimetres) to uranium radiohalos. Hundreds of millions of years of decay are supposed to have been required for the formation of the uranium radiohalos. There is strong evidence that the polonium was transported from the uranium halo centres by fluids moving along the cleavages between the host biotite sheets. It's extremely intriguing that all the polonium isotopes have very short half-lives: 164 microseconds, 3.1

minutes and 138 days for ^{214}Po, ^{218}Po and ^{210}Po respectively. Consequently, the polonium radiohalos had to have formed within days of the uranium radiohalos; yet the polonium in the polonium radiohalos was supposed to result from hundreds of millions of years of uranium decay! There is an obvious and gigantic incompatibility here that imposes a large question mark over the long-age scenario.

Fission tracks are another visible record of radioactivity in rocks. The tracks are formed when a radioactive atom, usually uranium, splits into two smaller atoms. On rare occasions, uranium-238 undergoes fission to produce two palladium-119 atoms. As the two heavy atoms fly apart, they produce a track of significant damage to the crystal structure. These fission tracks are mostly observed in ceramics and glasses as microscopic tubes 0.01–0.015 millimetres in length. Fission tracks are also fragile, and fade on heating at 50–400°C depending on the mineral. Rock age determinations are frequently made from counts of the fission tracks in measured samples of suitable ceramics. Discriminating between genuine and pseudo tracks can cause problems.

The persistence of radiohalos and fission tracks in crystalline rocks from all sections of the geologic column reveals that their host materials have not experienced significant heating since their deposition. Both types of defects are delicate and disappear rapidly on heating. Radiohalo- and fission-track-containing minerals of Cambrian and Precambrian age would have experienced hundreds of millions of intense geologic episodes (see page 9). The fact of their persistence into the present is further evidence that these rocks are much younger than commonly supposed.

Conventional Age Determinations: The Default Mode

If radiometric methods are as flawed and unreliable as implied by the evidence reviewed so far, it's valid to ask why rock and fossil ages always seem to conform well to the limits assigned in the conventional geologic column. Why has this remained so little changed since the 1950s, as Figure 1.2 illustrates? Consideration of the way rocks, minerals and fossils are normally dated explains that this consistency is the preordained outcome. The stratigraphy of the specimen in question is first examined to determine its ranking in the geologic column. Specimens collected for dating rock units are invariably from volcanic rocks, such as basalt lava flows or volcanic ash beds that don't contain fossils. The stratigraphic age of such volcanic layers is thus initially determined from the suites of fossils in layers above and below them. The specimen will then be assigned an approximate age based on the time span of its period or sub-period in the geologic column. Specimens may then be sent for more precise dating by one or more of the radiometric methods outlined above. If an age outside the limits defined by its position in the geologic column is obtained, this will routinely be taken as evidence that the sample was unsuitable. The data will be discounted or 'reinterpreted' in some way. For results that appear too old, mixing with older material from the mantle or elsewhere will be presumed. If the radiometric age appears too young, loss of the daughter element by diffusion out or dissolution into moving groundwater or hydrothermal fluids will be invoked.

Only dates that are concordant with the established column can survive this selection process. The conventional geologic timescale enjoys such scientific prestige and is backed by such a weight of expert opinion that it always trumps contrary evidence.

This methodology ensures the protection and continuity of the conventional Deep Time scale. It's obvious, however, that this is an ideal system for rampant, mostly unconscious confirmation bias on the part of participating scientists.

Confirmation Bias

Confirmation bias, and the related phenomenon of 'experimenter expectancy' – seeing what you want to see – are pervasive problems in science. Researchers know that 'right' answers and positive outcomes have a far better chance of being published. While testing a cherished theory, the experimenter may unconsciously reject points he regards as 'outliers' for 'technical' reasons. He may unconsciously stop or start measurements in such a way as to favour the theory, believing extraneous factors are legitimately being eliminated. Figure 1.4 pictures this process at work.

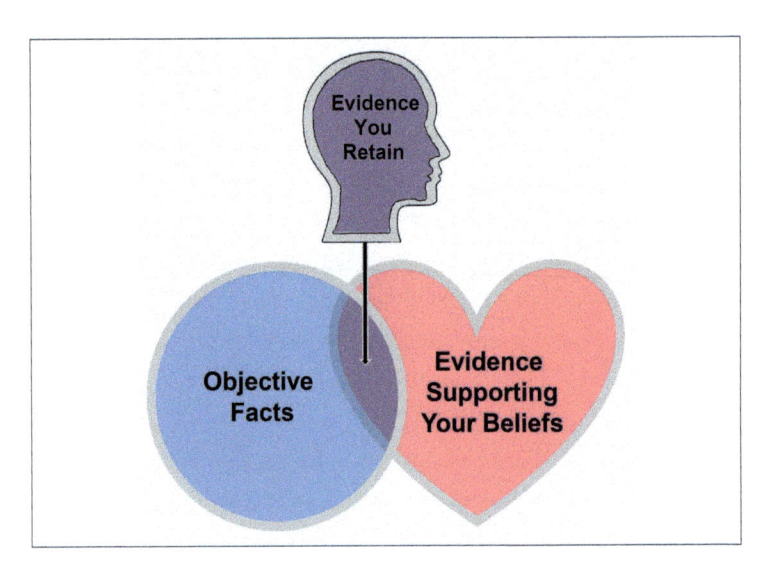

Figure 1.4 *Confirmation Bias.*

The prevalence of such self-deception in science has been demonstrated numerous times by psychological studies. For example, at Harvard, Robert Rosenthal asked a group of students to test two sets of rats. One set, they were told, were 'maze-bright' and had been specially trained to run mazes. The other set were 'maze-dull' and rather stupid. In fact, both sets had been randomly chosen from standard lab rats. However, the students' experiments found that the 'maze-bright' rats did significantly better! The real difference was in the students' expectations, and they unconsciously biased the outcome. Rosenthal's studies also showed how teachers' expectations were unconsciously biased by information they were fed about their pupils' IQs.

Broad and Wade, in their intriguing book *Betrayers of the Truth*, describe many actual instances, some tragic, some amusing, of this phenomenon at work in scientific research.[23] Self-deception of this sort on the part of palaeontologists played a major role in the notorious Piltdown affair. Research projects on animal language have been particularly fraught with experimenter bias. Researchers' evolution-inspired expectations of significant animal-to-man dialogue fed into absurd mistaken outcomes. At the University of Nevada, the Gardners taught their chimpanzee Washoe sign language. These signing apes became a flourishing subfield of psychological research in the 1970s. Researchers formed emotional bonds with their subject animals, and believed their chimps were developing large vocabularies and even stringing signs together in sentences. Herbert Terrace found his chimp Nim Chimpsky (named in honour of the distinguished linguist Noam Chomsky) learned signs extremely well and could make them into strings. However, Nim's strings never developed much sense. They were just successions of signs, as Nim's longest string demonstrates: "Give orange me give eat orange me eat orange give me eat orange give me you." Terrace eventually decided Nim's and the other chimps' strings were not true language. Critics claimed the chimps were simply imitating their teachers, and by the 1980s the research began to fall into disrepute and to be characterised as self-deception.

The pervasiveness of confirmation bias has led to the insistence on 'double-blind' experiments in clinical research. Neither the doctor nor the patient must know whether the drug is a placebo or otherwise. Unfortunately, this practice hasn't become universal in science. Double-blind studies are rare in radiometric dating. Research projects were described above where samples were sent for isochron dating without any indication of their provenance. The erratic results strongly suggest that confirmation bias is indeed endemic in this area too.

Naturally, the filtering process behind radiometric chronological data isn't normally reported, but occasional glimpses of it appear. There is, for example, an amusing chapter in the saga of the Leakey family's Lake Turkana (formerly Lake Rudolf) explorations.[24] Richard Leakey's team were discovering fossil hominid bones in the Koobi Fora Formation along the east shore of Lake Turkana in northern Kenya. Kay Behrensmeyer, then a Harvard graduate student, discovered a volcanic ash layer (named the KBS Tuff after her) that could be used for radiometric dating. Samples were sent to Jack Miller at Cambridge University, who worked in collaboration with Bill Bishop of Bedford College, London. They used K-Ar dating to obtain an initial age of 220 million years. Deciding that these samples were 'obviously' unsuitable, more were sent and dated to 2.61 Ma BP by the more sophisticated ^{40}Ar-^{39}Ar method. A year or so later, at a conference in Nairobi, Miller and Fitch presented forty-one separate age determinations on the KBS Tuff which varied between 223 and 0.91 Ma BP. They simply discounted all the samples with ages they considered too old or too young on the grounds of contamination or degassing. They steadfastly maintained over many years that their 2.61 Ma BP date was "incontrovertible".

However, evolution theory data conflicting with this date began to appear. Palaeontologist Basil Cooke, also working at the Koobi Fora site, made a study of the evolution of pig fossil molar teeth. He showed that the Koobi Fora pig teeth matched younger ones from neighbouring sites dated around 2 Ma BP, thereby throwing doubt on the 2.61 Ma BP date of the KBS Tuff. A year or two later Richard Leakey announced the discovery of the famous ER 1470 skull from below the "securely dated" KBS Tuff. Large sections of the palaeoanthropology community believed ER 1470 was much too similar to the skulls of *Homo sapiens* to be as old as 2.61 Ma BP; implying again that there was a serious problem with the KBS Tuff dating. Around this time, Glynn Isaac and Andrew Brock made a study of palaeomagnetic reversals in rocks above and below the KBS Tuff. Their data, however, indicated a date of about 2.6 Ma BP in support of the Miller/Fitch result!

Garniss Curtis, a geochronologist at Berkeley, California, was convinced the KBS Tuff must be younger. He obtained fresh samples of Tuff material and proceeded to date them by the conventional K-Ar method. He proposed that there were two Tuffs, and that both were much younger. He reported K-Ar ages of 1.6 and 1.8 Ma BP. Although Curtis's method was older and less reliable, his dates were much more acceptable to the palaeoanthropological community, for whom early *Homo* was anathema. The controversy raged on and took centre stage at a succession of scientific symposia.

The next development in the story concerned Anthony Hurford, a student of Fitch's in London who, together with Andrew Gleadow, worked on fission-track dating of KBS Tuff samples. Gleadow wrote, "After a critical assessment of all the data now in hand, I am convinced that a fission track of 2.4 m.y. for the KBS tuff... is quite inescapable."[25] Shortly after the publication of the fission-track data, Miller and Fitch communicated a further ^{40}Ar-^{39}Ar study, with updated decay constants, that agreed very well with the fission-track result. They contended that Curtis's samples had suffered from argon loss, giving a date younger than the actual date of the Tuff. Curtis, on the other hand, maintained that the samples dated by Miller and Fitch were probably contaminated with argon from older inclusions.

Year	Dating Team	Method	KBS Tuff Age (Ma BP)
1969	Miller & Fitch	K-Ar	220
1970	Miller & Fitch	^{40}Ar-^{39}Ar	2.61±0.26
1971	Cooke & Maglio	Fossil pig molars	2.0
1974	Isaac & Brock	Palaeomagnetism	2.6
1975	Curtis	K-Ar	1.6 & 1.8
1975	Hurford & Gleadow	Fission tracks	2.44±0.08
1976	Miller & Fitch	^{40}Ar-^{39}Ar	2.42±0.01
1980	Hurford & Gleadow	Fission tracks	1.8
1980, 1985	McDougall	K-Ar & fission tracks	1.9

Table 1.3: *Controversial Dating of the Lake Turkana KBS Tuff.*

However, evolutionary anthropologists weighed in heavily on the side of younger dates for the KBS Tuff. Don Johanson and Tim White were promoting 'Lucy' and *Australopithecus afarensis* as the ultimate human ancestor. These australopithecine skulls, dated at around 3 Ma BP, were small-brained with heavy brow ridges, and were altogether very ape-like. In evolutionary terms this was incompatible with the much larger, smooth-browed ER 1470 individual being around at about 2.9 Ma BP, as Leakey then maintained.

The young Gleadow visited Curtis at Berkeley. He and Hurford also attended several conferences where they listened to the palaeoanthropologists' doubts about the antiquity of the KBS Tuff. They decided on a recount of the fission tracks in their KBS Tuff samples. It's no surprise that they then arrived at the younger age of 1.8 Ma BP! Richard Leakey was ill, and weary of a controversy he saw as detrimental to his health and professional standing. He arranged for Ian McDougall, a respected geochronologist from the Australian National University, to gather a team, collect more samples and arrive at a final solution. They used K-Ar and fission-track dating to arrive at a date of 1.9 Ma BP. Richard Leakey wrote that, "It was only in 1980... that a broad consensus was finally achieved."

What the dates in Table 1.3 actually show are ranges of data broad enough to permit several different opinions. It's difficult to avoid the conclusion that confirmation bias played a substantial role. Furthermore, the final accepted outcome seems to have been more influenced by evolution theory than by the supposedly precise experimental determinations. Of the latter, only those conforming to current theories about human and pig evolution found eventual acceptance. A healthy scepticism should be maintained in regard to published geochronological dates. Inherently, there are many sources of error. The final column of Table 2.1 shows that different methods produced ages way outside the error limits attached to individual data points. The KBS Tuff saga illustrates the crucial role played by the subjective judgements of the individual research workers at multiple stages – first in the selection of specimens deemed suitable for study, then in selecting which dates to discard from the spread obtained, and then in assessing the role of contamination or loss of daughter products. The researchers' expectations and preconceptions, strongly coloured by prevailing theory, inevitably influenced these judgements.[26]

An objective, uncommitted observer would be bound to see Deep Time as an edifice of eggshell fragility. It's held together by an extensive grid of confirmation bias, grounded on evolutionary theory tied to methodological naturalism.

Chapter 1: References and Notes

1. A. S. Eddington, *The Nature of the Physical World*, 1927, pp. 328–9; *The Nature of the Physical World*, University of Michigan 1981 edition.
2. James Hutton, *Theory of the Earth*, 1785.
3. Charles Lyell, *Principles of Geology*, first edition 1930, twelfth edition 1875, London.
4. Arthur Holmes, *The Age of the Earth*, Nelson, London, 1937, p. 37.
5. A. Holmes, ibid., p. 164.
6. A. Holmes, ibid., p. 155.
7. A. Holmes, ibid., p. 174.
8. Arthur Holmes, *Principles of Physical Geology* (new and fully revised edition), Nelson, London, 1965, pp. 15–7.
9. The ICS timescale can be viewed at: https://stratigraphy.org/chart (Accessed 6th September 2020).
10. See for example F. Albarède, *Geochemistry: An Introduction*, second edition, Cambridge University Press, Cambridge, 2009.
11. A. A. Snelling, 'The cause of anomalous potassium-argon "ages" for recent andesite flows at Mt. Ngauruhoe, New Zealand and the implications for potassium-argon dating' in R. E. Walsh (ed.), *Proceedings of the Fourth International Conference on Creationism*, Creation Science Fellowship, Pittsburgh, Pennsylvania, 1998, pp. 503–25.
12. L. Vardiman, A. A. Snelling and E. F. Chaffin (eds.), *Radioisotopes and the Age of the Earth*, Institute of Creation Research, El Cajon, California, and St. Joseph, Missouri, 2000.
13. J. Mason, 'Radiometric Dating' in *Evolution's Achilles' Heels*, R. Carter (ed.), Creation Book Publishers, 2014, pp. 193–213.
14. A. A. Snelling, 'Isochron discordances, inheritance and mixing' in *Radioisotopes and the Age of the Earth*, Volume II, L. Vardiman, A. A. Snelling and E. F. Chaffin (eds.), Institute of Creation Research, El Cajon, California, and Creation Research Society, Chiro Valley, Arizona, 2005, 393–524.
15. D. DeYoung, *Thousands Not Billions*, Master Books, 2005, Ch. 8, pp. 123–39.
16. S. Austin, *Grand Canyon: Monument to Catastrophe*, Institute of Creation Research, Dallas, 1994, p. 126.

17. A. A. Snelling, *Earth's Catastrophic Past*, Volume 2, Institute of Creation Research, Dallas, 2009, pp. 797–838.
18. Y. F. Zheng, 'Influences of the nature of the initial rubidium-strontium system on isochron validity' in *Chemical Geology*, 1989, *80*, pp. 1–16.
19. See for example (a) G. Faure and J. L. Powell, *Strontium Isotope Geology*, Springer-Verlag, Berlin, 1972; (b) T. S. McCarthy and R. G. Cawthorn, 'Changes in initial $^{87}Sr/^{86}Sr$ ratio during protracted fractionation in igneous complexes' in *Journal of Petrology*, 1980, *21*, pp. 245–64.
20. (a) H. Köhler and D. Müller-Sohnius, 'Rb-Sr systematics on paragneiss series from Bavarian Moldanubian, Germany' in *Contributions to Mineralogy and Petrology*, 1980, 71, pp. 387–92; (b) U. Haack, J. Hoefs and E. Gohn, 'Constraints on the origin of Damaran granites by Rb/Sr and $d^{18}O$ data' in *Contributions to Mineralogy and Petrology*, 1982, *79*, pp. 279–89.
21. A. P. Dickin, *Radiogenic Isotope Geology*, second edition, Cambridge University Press, Cambridge, UK, 2005.
22. A. A. Snelling, *Earth's Catastrophic Past*, Volume 2, Institute of Creation Research, Dallas, 2009, pp. 837–43.
23. W. Broad and N. Wade, *Betrayers of the Truth*, Oxford University Press, 1985, Ch. 6, pp. 107–25.
24. R. Lewin, *Bones of Contention*, Simon & Schuster, New York, 1987, pp. 189–252.
25. Letter from Gleadow to R. Leakey, 15th March 1976, quoted in R. Lewin, p. 243.
26. For a germane critique of radiometric dating see C. Rupe and J. C. Sanford, *Contested Bones*, FMS Publications, 2007, p. 269 et seq.

Chapter 2

The Extraordinary Pervasiveness Of Radiocarbon

> *Life exists in the universe only because the carbon atom possesses certain exceptional properties.*
> James Jeans

> *An adopted hypothesis gives us lynx-eyes for everything that confirms it and makes us blind to everything that contradicts it.*
> Arthur Schopenhauer

The Radiocarbon Time Domain: A New Prospect

Carbon is the most uninhibited of the elements. It enters relationships with practically every other known element. Its compounds take on every possible shape, form and structure. Carbon ranks only fifteenth in abundance in the Earth's crust, but it connects so naturally with everything else that its influence is unrivalled. Nowhere is it more important than in the world of living things. Atmospheric carbon dioxide is at the top of the food chain because of its role in photosynthesis. Carbon accounts for 18.5% by weight of the human body. Proteins, carbohydrates, lipids and nucleic acids all exist and function because of carbon.

Specialised carbon compounds are even at work in our thinking processes. Our ability to rationally reflect on the roles of carbon depends on carbon compounds! Carbon is also widespread in the environment. Plants, trees, coal, oil, shale, limestone, chalk, marble, and many other substances from animate and seemingly inanimate sources all contain much carbon. The exceptionally wide distribution of carbon makes it very promising as a basis for geochronology.

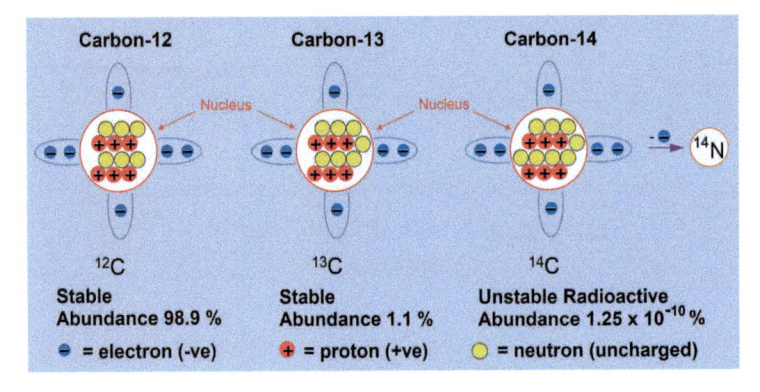

Figure 2.1: *Graphic Representation of the Isotopes of Carbon.*

More than anyone else, Willard Libby was the pioneer in the development of radiocarbon dating. He began his research career at Berkeley in the 1930s by developing and making sensitive Geiger counters to measure weak radioactivity. Then during World War II, he served in the notorious Manhattan Project at Columbia University, building hardware for uranium enrichment. After the war, Libby accepted a chair at the University of Chicago where he discovered the ingenious carbon-based radiometric method of timing. The main form of this element in nature is the isotope carbon-12 (^{12}C) with six protons and six neutrons in its nucleus. Carbon compounds also contain small amounts (about 1.1%) of another isotope, carbon-13 (^{13}C), with an extra neutron in its nucleus as depicted in Figure 2.1. Libby was aware that carbon also possesses in very minute amounts a further isotope, carbon-14 (^{14}C), with two extra neutrons. Crucially, this isotope is unstable and decays radioactively. The half-life is only 5,730 years, so a ten-gram sample of ^{14}C decays to five grams in 5,730 years, to 2.5 grams in 11,460 years, and down to 0.01 grams in ten half-lives, i.e. 57,300 years (Figure 2.2).

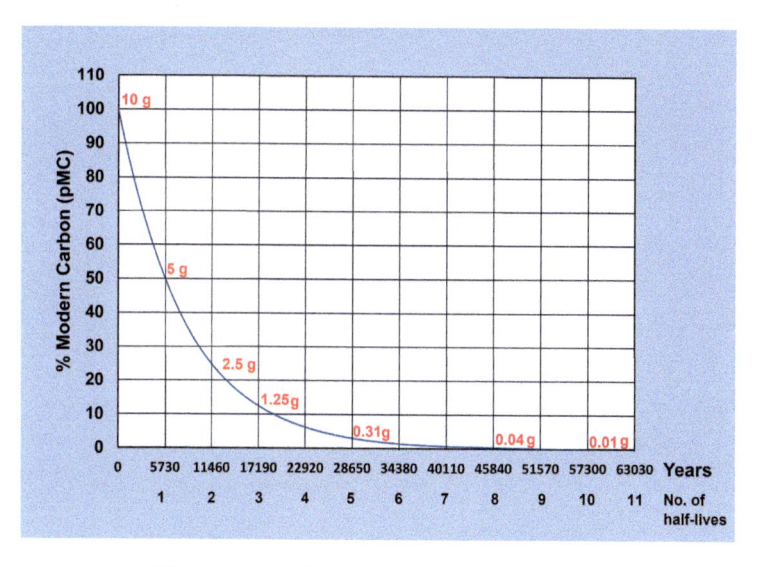

Figure 2.2: *Radioactive Decay of Carbon-14.*

He learned that this radiocarbon is constantly being formed in the Earth's atmosphere. Cosmic rays interact with the atmosphere to produce neutrons which react with nitrogen-14 (^{14}N), the main component of the atmosphere, to release the carbon-14. The ^{14}C rapidly combines with oxygen to produce radioactively labelled carbon dioxide. Plants absorb this during photosynthesis and it's passed to animals that eat the plants. The ingested ^{14}C continually undergoes radioactive decay back to nitrogen-14 but, while alive, plants and animals constantly replenish their supply of ^{14}C from the atmosphere. Thus, an equilibrium is reached whereby the ^{14}C content in plants and animals throughout the biosphere remains constant. When they die, no more labelled carbon dioxide is taken in so, from then onwards, the amount of ^{14}C in their carcasses decreases according to the exponential radioactive decay law (Figure 2.3).

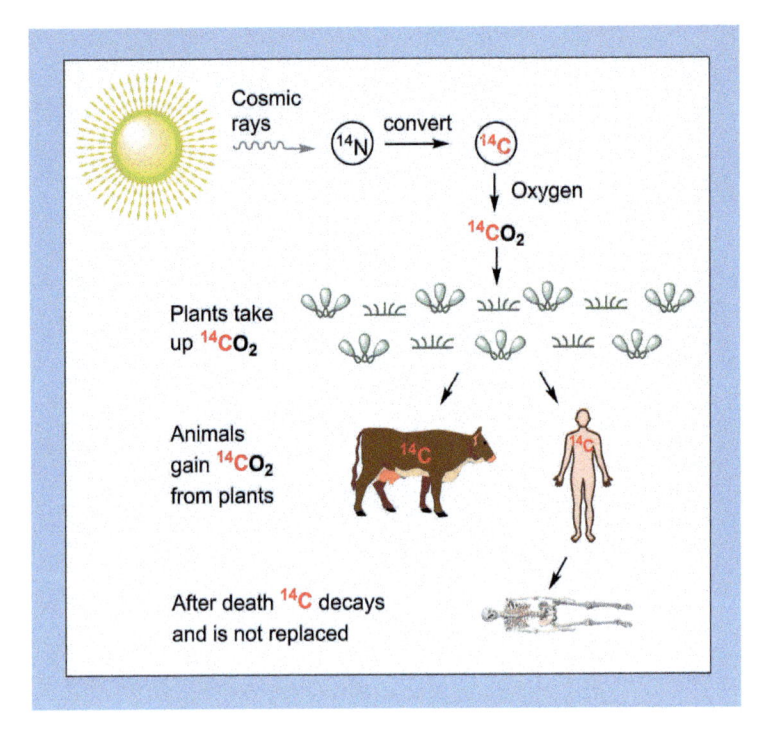

Figure 2.3: *Principle of Radiocarbon Dating.*

Libby recognised that by measuring the amount of ^{14}C in a specimen, the time elapsed since the animal or plant died could be determined.

Of course, the method depends on knowing the proportion of ^{14}C in the atmosphere and biosphere; that's the $^{14}C/C$ ratio (C is the sum of $^{12}C + {}^{13}C$). Libby's first dating experiments assumed this had remained constant over the measurable time frame. However, evidence steadily accumulated showing that variations had taken place. The burning of fossil fuels and the nuclear tests in the 1950s and '60s substantially affected the atmospheric $^{14}C/C$ level. Furthermore, there were some comparatively small variations due to differential uptake by different organisms, and due to different proportions in certain areas of the biosphere. Ways of correcting for these effects – some good, others questionable – were devised and are now routinely applied.

The half-life of ^{14}C is 'only' 5,730 years; that's very much shorter than the half-lives of uranium, potassium and the other elements of isochron dating. Fortunately for us, the initial equilibrium amount of ^{14}C in the atmosphere and in living species is extremely small, otherwise our bodies would be seriously damaged by radiation! In the biosphere there are only about 1.25 atoms of ^{14}C for every trillion atoms of ^{12}C. Expressed as a percentage, this is extremely minute at $^{14}C/C = 1.25 \times 10^{-10}$ %. Every ten half-lives (around fifty-seven thousand years) this ratio decreases further in dead material by a factor of 1,024. Beta-counting devices (Geiger counters) available to Libby counted the amount of beta radiation emitted by the decaying ^{14}C atoms in a sample. The tiny amounts of ^{14}C were very difficult to measure with these counters. More recently, accelerator mass spectrometry (AMS) has become the method of choice; it counts *all* the ^{14}C atoms in a sample, not just the few that happen to decay during the period of measurement, and so is inherently more sensitive. AMS can therefore be used with much smaller samples (as small as individual plant seeds) and gives results much more quickly.

The minuscule amount of ^{14}C remaining in a specimen after one hundred thousand years or more of decay would be beyond the limits of detection of even the most sensitive modern AMS spectrometers. In nature, therefore, any carbon-containing substance older than this should have no detectable ^{14}C. In practical terms, most radiocarbon dating is actually confined to specimens less than sixty thousand years old. Samples that are one million years or older should certainly contain no radiocarbon at all. It was expected, therefore, that the geological range of applicability of radiocarbon dating would be restricted to specimens of recent and Late Quaternary age. Rocks and fossils from the majority of the geologic column were confidently predicted to be radiocarbon 'dead'.

Before the half-life of ^{14}C had been accurately measured, Libby and other early radiocarbon exponents used a half-life of 5,568 years, and consequently many early radiocarbon dates (prior to about 1960) reflect this. It was also soon realised that in fact, the level of ^{14}C in the atmosphere had experienced small fluctuations over time. Ways of trying to correct for this were devised, mostly based on tree-ring observations. Calibration curves to convert the measured ^{14}C in a sample into a more reliable estimate of calendar age were developed. Modern radiocarbon dating still uses the Libby half-life, but the calibration curves correct for this. Most modern radiocarbon dates are therefore reported as 'calibrated'.

As a check on its validity, radiocarbon dating has frequently been tested with specimens of wood and with archaeological artefacts of known age. The method isn't capable of measuring ages to an accuracy of one year but, for well-preserved samples, error limits can be ±20 to ±100 years depending on the age. With this qualification, the method was found to perform very well when dating materials of up to about 3,000 BP. For items older than this, i.e. for Bronze Age and Stone Age specimens of known provenance, many serious disagreements surfaced between ^{14}C ages and those deduced from historical and archaeological data. Much confusion developed around the chronologies of Near Eastern, Middle Eastern and other civilisations of these time periods. A vexed controversy grew up amongst historians, archaeologists and radiocarbon chronologists regarding the validity of radiocarbon dates for specimens and events from these eras. The problem remains unresolved to this day, and alternative chronologies for affected civilisations appear in the literature from time to time. This subject is addressed in more detail in Chapter 5.

Radiocarbon dating has become an invaluable aid in the forensic science of antique and archaeological objects no older than about 3000 years. Its roles in authenticating the Dead Sea Scrolls and in assigning a date from 210–45 BC to the Great Isaiah Scroll are well known. Laboratories in many countries are engaged in applying radiocarbon dating to the authentication of antiques and historical items supposedly of medieval, Roman, ancient Egyptian, antique Chinese, and other provenance. An intriguing case is that of the Turin Shroud. Radiocarbon dating provided a medieval age of AD 1,260–1,390,[1] although this continues to be challenged on various grounds. The controversy over the authenticity of the Vinland Map, showing Greenland and lands west of this, was settled by radiocarbon dating. This gave the map's date as AD 1,411–1,464; about half a century before Columbus's voyage. Radiocarbon is also a key technique in detecting the illegal trade in modern ivory posing as antique ivory.

Radiocarbon Permeates the Whole Geologic Column

Scientists always push their techniques to their ultimate limit and beyond. In this way new horizons may be glimpsed, and new discoveries made. This was certainly true of radiocarbon dating. Materials of greater and greater antiquity continued to be examined. Amongst Deep Time advocates it was axiomatic that ancient carbon would be radio-dead. In fact, ancient coal and charcoal samples had been routinely used as calibration blanks. Radiocarbon detected with these reference blanks was assumed to be background interference and was subtracted from the results obtained from specimens under study. It was very surprising and disquieting, therefore, when AMS results began to appear showing small but significant amounts of ^{14}C in ancient coal and other pre-Pleistocene materials.

Contamination of some sort was taken to be the likely explanation, so extensive experimentation was undertaken to locate the source. It was established that AMS instrument background was negligible for properly serviced spectrometers. Contamination by modern carbon did occur in some specimens but, provided they were judiciously selected, properly cleaned and processed, this could be ruled out. Some contamination could be introduced if processing of specimens was not carefully planned and supervised. However, this could not account for the amounts found. Another suggestion was that ^{14}C might be generated by nuclear reactions taking place while the samples were in the ground. Various lines of evidence have shown this is most improbable.[2] A flux of neutrons could convert the ^{13}C in fossils to ^{14}C but, because this decays with a half-life of only 5,730 years, the neutron flux would have to recur many times for fossils millions of years old. Furthermore, most organic material contains ^{14}N, and this captures neutrons orders of magnitude more easily than carbon. If neutron capture were significant, then the ^{14}C content of fossils would vary depending on their nitrogen content, contrary to the facts.

Many laboratories in different countries have reported finding significant ^{14}C in ancient, pre-Pleistocene materials as diverse as wood, coal, anthracite, graphite, bone, marble, calcite and natural gas.[3] Paul Giem tabulated about seventy such reports, all from the academic radiocarbon literature, indicating ^{14}C levels above the AMS instrumental background.[2] His compilation includes organic samples from essentially every stratum of the geologic column down to the Precambrian. The amounts reported varied from about 0.5–0.1 pMC, where pMC (percent modern carbon) refers to the ^{14}C/C ratio in the fossil expressed as a percentage of the same ratio existing in the atmosphere, by convention in 1950, before nuclear tests disturbed it. These residual ^{14}C/C ratios translate to 'young' ages in the range 44,000–57,000 BP.

If these radiocarbon amounts in all these fossils were attributable to contamination, then it would be expected that they would have diminished over time as laboratory techniques for sample preparation and handling improved. However, Giem's plots of the reported results showed no discernible trend with time. Experiments in which the sample size was varied by large factors also supported the conclusion that the ^{14}C was intrinsic to the fossil material and not a result of handling or pretreatment. It's a fact that organic materials from all periods of the geologic column down to the bottom of the Cambrian are regularly found to contain ^{14}C levels well above instrumental background, even after extreme pretreatments.[4]

Geochronologists and palaeontologists still routinely dismiss the ^{14}C discovered in organic materials from Tertiary and older strata as 'contamination'. Before accepting this verdict, it should be noted that when radiocarbon laboratories report ^{14}C *at these same levels* (0.5–0.1 pMC) in specimens from ancient Stone Age cultures, contamination is not called upon. For example, radiocarbon analyses of artefacts from Mousterian-type cultures of the Middle Palaeolithic in France and the Mediterranean yielded ^{14}C/C ratios in the range 2.6–0.13 pMC, corresponding to ages in the range 30,000–55,000 BP.[5] Similarly, materials from Middle Palaeolithic sites in Israel, Syria and Lebanon gave ^{14}C/C from 1.45–0.30 pMC, from which dates of 35,000–48,000 BP were deduced. The genuineness of these results went unquestioned and the corresponding ages were received as historically accurate. These are just a few of the many radiocarbon dates from prehistoric sites that are accepted without demur. The specimens from much more ancient, Tertiary, pre-Pleistocene strata were cleaned, carefully processed and measured by professionals using the same techniques. Why then insist that the ^{14}C they contain, in comparable amounts, must be contamination? It's incoherent to arbitrarily reject the same data in one situation, but uncritically allow it in another. For consistency, the ^{14}C/C ratios from Middle Palaeolithic sites would also have to be dismissed as contamination, making their dates fictitious.

Location	Coal Seam	Conventional Age (Ma BP)	^{14}C/C (pMC ± 1σ)	^{14}C Age[a] (Years BP)
Texas	Bottom	34–55	0.30±0.03	48,000
N. Dakota	Beulah	34–55	0.20±0.02	51,400
Montana	Oust	34–55	0.27±0.02	48,900
Utah	Lower Sunnyside	65–145	0.35±0.03	46,700
Utah	Blind Canyon	65–145	0.10±0.03	57,100
Arizona	Green	65–145	0.18±0.02	52,200
Kentucky	Kentucky #9	300–311	0.46±0.03	44,500
Pennsylvania	Lykens Valley	300–311	0.13±0.02	54,900
Pennsylvania	Pittsburgh	300–311	0.19±0.02	51,800
Illinois	Illinois #6	300–311	0.29±0.03	48,300

[a] *Uncalibrated ages based on ^{14}C half-life of 5,730 years.*

Table 2.1: *Measured Carbon-14 in Ancient Coal Samples.*[4, 6]

DeYoung described a remarkable study of a set of coal samples.[4,6,7] Coals from the Palaeozoic, Mesozoic and Cenozoic eras of the geologic column were obtained from the Coal Sample Bank of the US Department of Energy. Their ^{14}C content was measured with the AMS method by a reputable commercial laboratory (Table 2.1). Every coal sample exhibited residual ^{14}C significantly above instrumental error. The average ^{14}C/C ratios of 0.26, 0.21 and 0.27 pMC for the coals from the Cenozoic, Mesozoic and Palaeozoic eras respectively displayed no trend in relation to their conventional ages. There is really no basis for attributing such sizeable amounts of ^{14}C to 'contamination'. If the residual ^{14}C found in these coals resulted from decay of initial ^{14}C equal to that in the present atmosphere, this implies drastically younger ages than their geological eras indicate. The radiocarbon ages calculated with these assumptions are in the final column and range from only about 44,000–58,000 BP.

Figure 2.4: *Coal Seams of the Permian Galilee Basin, Queensland.*
Image: Lee Prince, Shutterstock.com

A study of the ^{14}C content of diamonds obtained from South and West Africa produced another interesting result.[6] Diamonds are thought to originate in the Earth's mantle and to be billions of years old (Ga). Twelve small industrial-quality diamonds were tested by the AMS technique and the average ^{14}C/C ratio was found to be 0.09±0.03 pMC. An instrumental 'background signal' of 0.08 pMC was subtracted to arrive at this result. AMS measurements of ^{14}C content were also carried out by another research group on natural diamonds, associated with Ceylon geological graphite, having conventional dates greatly in excess of 100 Ma.[8] These diamonds also had easily measurable ^{14}C corresponding to apparent ages in the range of 64,900–80,000 years. The evidence is therefore accumulating that the residual ^{14}C found in diamonds is not 'background' contamination. The implication is that diamonds also contain a low level of intrinsic ^{14}C and are much younger than their conventional ages. More data for diamonds from different locations and of diverse kinds is clearly desirable.

Radiocarbon and Dinosaurs

Ever since their discovery, dinosaurs have fascinated scientists, the public and particularly the entertainment industry. Each new finding seems to heighten the appeal of these fearsome creatures and draw in more interest. As soon as authentic reports of soft tissues in fossil dinosaur bones began to appear,[9,10] dinosaur remains soared high on the wish list for radiocarbon dating. The grim reluctance of mainstream science to undertake the work, or to publish the results, seems misguided. Opposition to such intriguing results was always going to be a losing battle! In due course, several independent sets of results were obtained from reputable laboratories and the internet provided a convenient outlet.

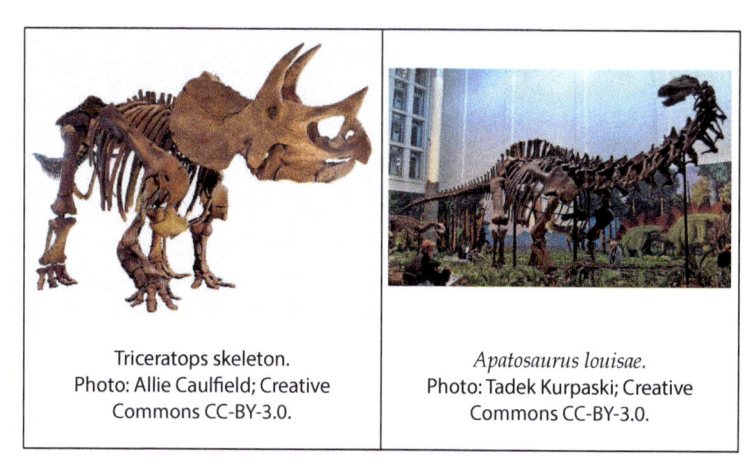

| Triceratops skeleton. Photo: Allie Caulfield; Creative Commons CC-BY-3.0. | *Apatosaurus louisae.* Photo: Tadek Kurpaski; Creative Commons CC-BY-3.0. |

Figure 2.5: *Mounted Fossils of Two Species of Dinosaur.*

Special care to avoid contamination was taken in the preparation of samples from dinosaur bones and tissues. The samples collected from the field were protected, cracked areas of bones were avoided and meticulous pre-cleaning was carried out. Collagen can attract contamination, but tests of samples of various sizes showed this was not a problem.

A selection from the results obtained by the Palaeochronology Groups of the US, France and Poland is shown in Table 2.2. They were presented in a talk at the 2012 Western Pacific Geophysics Meeting in Singapore, August 13th–17th, but are now only available on the internet.[11] All the specimens contained ^{14}C well above the instrumental background corresponding to the 'young' uncalibrated dates shown.

Location	Dinosaur	Era	Convent. Age (Ma BP)	^{14}C/C (pMC)	^{14}C Age (BP)
Texas	Acrosaurus	Cretaceous	65–150	<1.99	>32,400
Texas	Acrosaurus	Cretaceous	65–150	4.44	25,750
Colorado	Allosaurus	Late Jurassic	~150	2.25	31,360
Alaska	Hadrosaur 1	Cretaceous	65–150	3.34	31,050
Alaska	Hadrosaur 1	Cretaceous	65–150	1.21	36,480
Montana	Triceratops 1	Cretaceous	65–150	2.38	30,890
Montana	Triceratops 2	Cretaceous	65–150	0.87	39,230
Montana	Hadrosaur 2	Cretaceous	65–150	6.67	22,380
Colorado	Hadrosaur 3	Cretaceous	65–150	1.95	37,660
Colorado	Apatosaur	Late Jurassic	~150	0.98	38,250

Table 2.2: *Radiocarbon Dating of Dinosaur Fossils.*[11]

Thomas and Nelson obtained radiocarbon dates for a series of fossils including several dinosaurs.[12] A selection of their data for fossil bones from four dinosaur species is in Table 2.3. Again, all the diverse dinosaur specimen types yielded ^{14}C significantly above background readings.

Mark Armitage, originally a microscopist at California State University, discovered the unpetrified brow horn of a triceratops at the Hell Creek Formation in Montana. This became a cause célèbre because, following the publication in *Acta Histochemica* of his discovery of soft tissues in the fossil,[13,14] he was summarily fired from his post in the Biology Department. He was eventually awarded substantial damages for wrongful dismissal in an out-of-court settlement.[15]

Taxon	Stratigraphy Formation	¹⁴C/C pMC	¹⁴C Age BP	Specimen
Edmontosaurus	Lance	4.15	25,550	Vertebra
Edmontosaurus	Lance	1.77	32,420	Phalanx
Hadrosaur vert	Hell Creek	2.78	28,790	Cortical bone
Hadrosaur vert	Hell Creek	7.46	20,850	Medullary bone
Hadrosaur	Horseshoe Canyon	1.69	32,770	Caudal vertebra
Ceratopsian	Horseshoe Canyon	3.78	26,300	Metacarpal V
Ceratopsian	Horseshoe Canyon	1.03	36,760	Caudal vertebra
Triceratops	Hell Creek	1.53	33,570	Horn
Triceratops	Hell Creek	0.61	41,010	Horn

Table 2.3: *Radiocarbon Dates for Fossil Dinosaur Specimens.*[12]

Hugh Miller, head of the Palaeochronology Group, obtained a bone sample from the triceratops horn Mark Armitage had discovered. The sample was sent to the Center for Applied Isotope Studies at the University of Georgia in 2012 to test for carbon-14. Once again, the outcome (see Table 2.4) provided yet more evidence of substantial residual ¹⁴C in dinosaur bones.

Dinosaur	Formation	Conventional Age (Ma BP)	¹⁴C/C (pMC)	¹⁴C Age (BP)
Triceratops	Hell Creek	66	1.53	33,570

Table 2.4: *Radiocarbon Date for a Triceratops Horn.*

A Profound Challenge for Deep Time Chronology

The evidence is overwhelming for the presence of residual radiocarbon in carbon-containing materials from throughout the geologic column. Many palaeontologists and evolutionary scientists are unaware of or ignore this problem. Others contend it's simply due to 'contamination' from an unknown source. If so, it must be an especially lively type of contamination. That's because the half-life of radiocarbon is short on the geologic timescale, so it decays away comparatively quickly. For materials supposedly hundreds of millions of years old, the 'contamination' must either keep appearing as a constant but undetectable background flow, or in a series of fluxes repeated millions of times. Neither of these scenarios seems at all plausible.

If contamination by primordial radiocarbon is rife throughout the geologic column then contamination from unknown sources of other radio-elements must also be expected. The radioactive elements uranium, rubidium and samarium have very long half-lives, so only one 'pulse' of 'contaminating primordial material' would be needed. During its history the Earth's crust has been subjected to a vast array of terrestrial and cosmic ecological forces, impacts and high-energy events, some of known origin, others unknown. It is entirely possible that primordial radio-elements and/or daughter elements could have been created during one of these episodes. The effect would be to invalidate the radiometric dates obtained with these elements.

Chapter 2: References and Notes

1. P. E. Damon et al., 'Radiocarbon dating of the Shroud of Turin' in *Nature*, 1989, *337*, pp. 611–15.
2. P. Giem, 'Carbon-14 content of fossil carbon' in *Origins*, 2001, *51*, pp. 6–30.
3. R. L. Whitelaw, 'Time, life, and history in the light of 15,000 radiocarbon dates' in *Creation Research Society Quarterly*, 1970, *7*(1), pp. 56–71.
4. J. R. Baumgardner, '14-C evidence for a recent global flood and a young earth' in *Radioisotopes and the Age of the Earth: A Young-Earth Creationist Research Initiative*, L. Vardiman, A. A. Snelling and E. F. Chaffin (eds.), Institute for Creation Research, El Cajon, California, and Creation Research Society, St. Joseph, Missouri, 2005, Volume II, pp. 587–630.
5. See for example C. C. Barshay-Szmidt, L. Eizenberg and M. Deschamps, 'Radiocarbon (AMS) dating the classic Aurignacian, Proto-Aurignacian and Vasconian Mousterian at Gatzarria Cave (Pyrénées-Atlantiques, France)' in *Paléo: Revue D'Archéologie Préhistorique*, 2012, *23*, pp. 11–38.
6. J. R. Baumgardner, A. A. Snelling, D. R. Humphreys and S. A. Austin, 'Measurable ^{14}C in fossilized organic materials: confirming the young earth creation-flood model' in *Proceedings of the Fifth International Conference on Creationism*, R. L. Ivey Jr. (ed.), Pittsburgh, Pennsylvania, Creation Science Fellowship, pp. 127–47.
7. D. DeYoung, *Thousands Not Billions*, Master Books, Green Forest, Arkansas, 2005, Ch. 3, pp. 45–62.
8. R. E. Taylor and J. Southon, 'Use of natural diamonds to monitor ^{14}C AMS instrument backgrounds' in *Nuclear Instruments and Methods in Physics Research*, 2007, *259*, pp. 282–7.
9. R. Pawlicki and M. Nowogrodzka-Zagórska, 'Blood vessels and red blood cells preserved in dinosaur bones' in *Annals of Anatomy*, 1998, 180, pp. 73–7.
10. (a) M. H. Schweitzer, J. L. Wittmeyer, J. R. Horner and J. K. Toporski, 'Soft-tissue vessels and cellular preservation in *Tyrannosaurus rex*' in *Science*, 2005, *307*, pp. 1952–5; (b) M. H. Schweitzer, J. L. Wittmeyer and J. R. Horner, 'Soft tissue and cellular preservation in vertebrate skeletal elements from the

Cretaceous to the present' in *Proceedings: Biological Sciences*, 2007, *274 (1607)*, pp. 183–97; (c) M. H. Schweitzer, W. Zheng, C. L. Organ, R. Avci, Z. Suo, L. M. Freimark, V. S. Lebleu, M. B. Duncan, M. G. Vander Heiden, J. M. Neveu, W. S. Lane, J. S. Cottrell, J. R. Horner, L. C. Cantley, R. Kalluri and J. M. Asara, 'Biomolecular characterization and protein sequences of the Campanian hadrosaur *B. canadensis*' in *Science*, 2009, *324*, pp. 626–31.

11. Palaeochronology Group: see https://newgeology.us/presentation48.html (accessed June 2020).
12. B. Thomas and V. Nelson, 'Radiocarbon in dinosaur and other fossils' in *Creation Research Society Quarterly*, 2015, *51*, pp. 299–311; see https://creationresearch.org/wp-content/uploads/crsq-2015-volume-51-number-4.pdf
13. M. H. Armitage and K. L. Anderson, 'Soft sheets of fibrillar bone from a fossil of the supraorbital horn of the dinosaur *Triceratops horridus*' in *Acta Histochemica*, 2013, *115*, pp. 603–8.
14. M. H. Armitage, 'Soft bone material from a brow horn of a *Triceratops horridus* from Hell Creek Formation, Montana' in *Creation Research Society Quarterly*, 2015, *51*, pp. 248–58.
15. For a full account see https://www.christiantoday.com/article/christian-scientist-wins-court-case-gets-hefty-payout-after-getting-fired-for-challenging-evolution/97725.htm (accessed 29th December 2019).

CHAPTER 3

DOWNSIZING GEOLOGIC DEEP TIME

*Research is to see what everybody else has seen,
and to think what nobody else has thought.*
ALBERT SZENT-GYÖRGYI

*Science alone of all the subjects contains within itself the
lesson of the danger of belief in the infallibility of the greatest
teachers of the preceding generation.*
RICHARD P. FEYNMAN

MULTITUDES OF CATASTROPHES

During the 20th century, naturalism – the belief that only natural laws and forces operate in the universe – began to dominate as the cultural mindset amongst scientists. Science was so successful that naturalism mounted up from being merely the method whereby science operated, to become the default philosophical option. Supernatural and spiritual phenomena were to be excluded from all aspects of reality. Evolution, with its essential dependence on Deep Time, is the credo that enables philosophical naturalists to become "intellectually fulfilled".[1] Inflexible adherence to this world view has become a prime matter of faith in many scientific circles.

The prestige of science is so high that Deep Time has been taught with authority in schools, colleges and universities for many decades. Authoritative articles advocating Deep Time are everywhere found in geoscience and biology textbooks and in online databases. Superb videos of the world's most scenic and spectacular natural features are continually screened by the media and engagingly promote the same message. Museums and institutions proudly claim hundreds of millions of years for their rock and fossil specimens. The older a rock or fossil is thought to be, the greater is its prestige, its glamour, and its value. The effect of all this has been decades of Deep Time conditioning of the public. Vast ages have become deeply embedded in the fabric of the modern Western world view. We have become comfortable with this way of seeing rocks, strata, fossils, and all geological features. Furthermore, thinking outside this temporal box is now essentially taboo amongst a dominant academic elite.

Nevertheless, immense ages require immense extrapolations from the known present into the remote past. Recorded history only extends a few thousand years back. Writing was first invented about five thousand years ago. Inscribed records of any kind are not much older. Even one million years is *two hundred times* this. A billion years is *two hundred thousand times* recorded history into the past! Could extrapolations over such immense time periods be justified? Extrapolations outside ranges of observables are notoriously unreliable. Long-range weather forecasting provides a cautionary example! The longer the extrapolation, the greater the uncertainty and the higher the risk. Powerful reasons for believing that the uniformitarian methods underlying Deep Time are flawed were presented in Chapter 1.

Following the radiocarbon evidence outlined in Chapter

2 must lead to a radical reassessment of geochronology. The consequences in relation to the formation of the geologic column and its fossil contents are profound. Radiocarbon dating of rocks and fossils implies a timescale of only thousands of years of elapsed time since much of the geologic column was deposited. Strikingly, recent geology has been turning away from old-style uniformitarianism and has been adopting 'actualism'.[2,3] This admits the importance of many catastrophic events in the building of geologic features.[4,5] Catastrophic events are, by definition, of short duration.

Examples of catastrophic features now recognised in the geologic column include (a) widespread, continent-sized, rapidly water-deposited sedimentary strata; (b) erosion features due to massive floods; (c) vast, extensive igneous or magmatic rock formations; (d) huge fossil 'graveyards' of rapidly buried organisms in many places around the world; and (e) numerous, catastrophic mass extinctions. A detailed account of many of these features has been given by Snelling.[6]

More and more sedimentary layers deposited by turbidity currents, mudslides and slumps are being recognised. These downhill underwater currents of rapidly flowing, sediment-laden water are triggered by earthquakes and deposit turbidite layers. A turbidity current can deposit a turbidite more than a metre thick, as a huge expanse of sediment covering thousands of square kilometres, in only a few hours.[7] They were first observed on Grand Banks off the south coast of Newfoundland and were subsequently recognised in many places including the western Mediterranean.[8] Forty-one Holocene turbidity currents were noted along the thousand-kilometre plate boundary stretching from Northern California to mid Vancouver Island.[9] Taiwan is a hotspot for submarine turbidity currents as there are large amounts of sediment suspended in rivers and it is seismically active. Off Hawaii, giant underwater landslides have transported blocks of rock "tens of kilometres" in size more than fifty kilometres. Submarine landslides off the edge of Norway's continental shelf, known as the Storegga suite, consist of debris up to 450 metres thick, spread over a distance of eight hundred kilometres.[10] The proportion of the geologic column attributable to such slumps, landslides and turbidites remains a matter of dispute.

Roles for enormous floods in the formation of extensive erosional features are now widely accepted. The Channeled Scablands of Washington State imply floodwaters of magnitude greater than any observed in the present. They are now attributed to a cataclysmic flood (or floods) that swept across eastern Washington State. Several studies have proposed that the English Channel was caused by two major floods.[11]

Figure 3.1: *Upper Cretaceous Turbidites from the Point Loma Formation, San Diego, California.*
Photo by Eurico Zimbres; Creative Commons CC-BY-3.0.

Mass extinctions of flora and fauna are a recurring theme throughout the geologic column. Five major mass extinctions are widely acknowledged,[12-14] but at least twenty additional minor ones have also been invoked. The enormous impact the 'big five' had on Earth's ecosystem can be gathered from the fact that each event is reckoned to have wiped out 60–90% of all species. Trilobites disappeared during one of these extinctions in the Permian/Triassic period, and dinosaurs perished towards the end of the Cretaceous period. Debate continues about the causes of all the mass extinctions.[15] Vague statements appear suggesting extinctions result "when a biosphere under long-term stress undergoes a short-term shock". Three factors are often highlighted: flood basalt events, sea-level falls, and asteroid impacts.

The flood basalts are produced by giant volcanic eruptions that cover vast stretches of land, or ocean floor, with basalt lava. Flood basalts can extend to whole provinces, such as those of the Deccan Traps of India. These consist of multiple layers of basalt that together are more than 6,600 feet thick, cover an area of about two hundred thousand square miles, and have a volume of about two hundred thousand cubic miles. Rampino and Stothers cited eleven distinct flood basalt episodes creating large volcanic provinces, plateaus, and mountain ranges around the world.[16] Many more are recognised, such as the large Paraná Plateau in Brazil, the Karoo basalts of South Africa and Russia's Siberian Platform.[17]

The last of the 'big five' extinctions, called the K-Pg extinction (formerly the K/T extinction), is associated with the demise of the dinosaurs and the appearance of mammal fossils. Many scientists believe this extinction was due to an asteroid impact at Chicxulub in the Yucatán Peninsula of Mexico. Another popular theory associates it with the enormous volcanic eruptions which formed the Deccan Traps lava beds in India.

Fossil graveyards are another recurring feature in the geologic record around the world. More than 120 species of marine organisms are preserved in the famous Burgess Shale in the Canadian Rocky Mountains. The Thunder Bay Limestone, which stretches for hundreds of square miles, is an enormous fossil graveyard that is largely composed of the broken remains of billions of corals, crinoids, brachiopods and other marine organisms. Other huge fossil graveyards include the shale found at the Montceau Basin in central France, the Francis Creek shale in Illinois, the Monte San Giorgio Basin bituminous shales in Italy, the Cow Branch Formation in Virginia, the Santana Formation of Brazil and the Tepexi Limestone in Mexico.[18]

Figure 3.2: *Oviraptorosauria Skeletons.*
Photo courtesy of Gary Todd; Wikimedia Commons CC-BY-3.0.

The late Professor Derek Ager, formerly President of the British Geological Association, always remained a staunch advocate of Deep Time. In his books, however, he drew attention to numerous examples of fossils and geological deposits that could not have formed by any means other than sudden catastrophes or disasters that occurred in fleeting moments of time. He wrote:

> *It is obvious to me that the whole history of the earth is one of short sudden happenings with nothing much in particular in between. I have often been quoted for my comparison of earth history with the traditional life of a soldier that is, "long periods of boredom separated by short periods of terror."*[19]

Ager suggested there were "more gaps than record", and that "It may be said that earth history is not a record of what actually happened but is a record of what happens to have been preserved."[20]

Snelling's comments on this are worth quoting:

> *Or to put it another way, the bulk of geological time occurred during gaps in the record! Of course, this merely begs the question of how Ager and the conventional community know that the gaps in the record represent vast eons of time. If neither the gaps nor the eons of geological time claimed to be associated with them are in the rock record, then one is left only with a record of brief catastrophic processes.*[21]

A characteristic of catastrophic events is, of course, that their duration is short. The 'gaps' in the geological record correspond, therefore, on the Deep Time chronology, to huge expanses of time millions of years long.

A Composite All-in-One Giga-Geologic Catastrophe?

It is most likely that the residual radiocarbon found in all strata of the geologic column has formed in the perfectly normal way from radioactive decay of original carbon-14. The radical conclusion must be faced that the geological strata and their contents are very much younger than commonly supposed. This calls for a telescoping or compacting of the geologic timescale by many orders of magnitude. A new model, hereinafter referred to as the Compact Time model (CpT model) is needed. For a cataclysm of this enormity, 'giga-catastrophe' seems more appropriate than just 'mega-catastrophe'! Cutting out the 'gaps' in the geologic record, amounting to many millions of years, would go a long way to achieving this. Removing the empty gaps would have the effect of linking together in a connected sequence all the individual catastrophes. Almost all the catastrophic depositional and erosional features and processes referred to above – turbidites, rapid water-deposited strata, massive floods, fossil graveyards and giant volcanic eruptions – only require times that are very brief on the old geological timescale. This implies further substantial shortening of the time required for accumulation of the geologic column.

Some insights may be gained from consideration of modern catastrophes. These upheavals are never isolated occurrences. Some initial high-energy event, frequently an earth movement originating deep in the crust or from the mantle, triggers a whole succession of interrelated catastrophic episodes. Consider two such modern natural disasters. On Friday 11th March 2011, a Magnitude 9 earthquake took place about forty-three miles off the Tōhoku Peninsula of Japan. It was followed by many aftershocks, some still taking place two years later. The earthquake triggered powerful tsunami waves that reached heights of over 130 feet and travelled at speeds of up to 435 miles per hour. The earthquake moved Honshu (the main island of Japan) eight feet east. Initially, the earthquake caused sinking of part of Honshu's Pacific coast by up to a metre, but after about three years, the coast rose back up and kept on rising to exceed its original height. The waves swept up to ten miles inland and deposited an estimated twenty-four to twenty-five million tons of rubble and debris in Japan. The Sendai Plain was inundated, adding further sedimentary deposits to those already there from previous floods.

Figure 3.3: *Tōhoku Tsunami Aftermath, Sendai Airport.*
Photo courtesy of Mikio Ishiwatari and Junko Sagara;
Wikimedia Commons CC-BY-3.0.

It was reported that the reflection pulse from these surges travelled back across the Pacific, causing a twelve-to-twenty-four-inch surge in Japan about forty-eight hours after the earthquake. The rapidity of the successive episodes was astonishing. Residents of Sendai received only eight to ten minutes' warning, such that more than nineteen thousand were drowned or buried. This succession of events may be characterised as a geologic branching chain reaction initiated by a tectonic movement.

The devastating Mount St. Helens eruption in Washington State, USA illustrates a different type of catastrophe. It was preceded by two months of earthquakes and bulging of the mountain's north slope. Eventually, on the 18th May 1980 the north face of the mountain suddenly descended in a massive landslide. This opened the way for a high-pressure hot mix of lava and pulverised rock to suddenly explode northwards toward Spirit

Lake, overtaking the avalanching face. The landslide travelled at up to 155 miles per hour and moved across Spirit Lake's west arm. Some of the slide spilled over a ridge, but most of it moved thirteen miles down the North Fork Toutle River, filling its valley up to six hundred feet deep with avalanche debris. A canyon about one fortieth the size of the Grand Canyon, with steep hundred-foot sides and complete with rock layers, was cut in the Toutle River area in just a few days. An area of about twenty-four square miles was covered, and the total volume of the deposit was about 0.7 cubic miles. Thousands of animals were killed and rapidly

Figure 3.4: *Mount St. Helens Eruption Plume from the South.*
Photo by Mike Doukas; Wikimedia Commons CC-BY-3.0.

buried by the advancing avalanche. Millions of trees were blown down, totalling more than four billion board feet. A vast log mat, including many upright trees, formed on Spirit Lake. A huge ash column grew to a height of twelve miles above the expanding crater in less than ten minutes and spread into the stratosphere for ten hours. About 540 million tons of ash fell over an area of more than twenty-two thousand square miles.

Both the Mount St. Helens and the Tōhoku disasters exemplify runaway chain reactions. An initial high-energy event in the crust triggered further rapid crustal movements. These swiftly extended the area of influence, and in turn provoked massive trauma to adjacent aqueous and lithic geologic features. Branching of the catastrophe resulted in further large-scale erosional and depositional events. Massive amounts of crustal change were accomplished in very short times by the chains of linked events.

An analogous dynamic crustal event, but on a greatly magnified scale, can certainly be conceived of. The crustal transformations caused by such a geologic giga-chain reaction would, given sufficient magnitude, extend across the entire globe. All the individual catastrophic features that characterise the Earth's crust, from the Cambrian upwards, could be linked into this one megalithic event. Initiation could be by a continent-sized tectonic earth movement, or movements, several orders of magnitude greater in energy than the Tōhoku occurrence, probably with aftershocks in proportion. Tsunamis of extraordinary size would sweep right across neighbouring continents as giant floods. Pulses and reflection pulses of floodwater would continue for days, perhaps months. The land masses would simultaneously experience lateral and vertical motions. Land deformations including folding, faulting and mountain building would result. Such events would certainly be accompanied by massive volcanism.

Periods of sediment erosion and waterborne deposition would follow one another in rapid succession. Land and sea creatures would be irresistibly overwhelmed. Many would be buried by the sediment-laden waters, giving rise to various fossil graveyards. The scale would be such that numerous taxa of living organisms would be wiped out, and one 'mass extinction' would follow another as the inundations proceeded. The scale and rapidity of these events would explain the huge extent of many geological formations, their flat layering and conformable boundaries. The upright polystrate fossil trees that are found penetrating several strata in many locations would thereby be explained.

The volcanism triggered by the rise and fall of the land masses would also be on a global scale. Intrusive and extrusive igneous activity would result, giving rise to the extensive shields, platforms, basins, large igneous provinces and oceanic crust found in a wide range of geological settings.

As judged by the rapidity of the Tōhoku and Mount St. Helens models, the initial high-energy events might only take weeks or months. However, the after-effects would certainly continue, only gradually dying away, probably over hundreds of years. Judged by the Mount St. Helens eruption, the ash, dust and particulate clouds accompanying the volcanism would spread globally in the stratosphere. Volcanism on the scale implied by the immense flood basalts would certainly cause ocean warming. Greatly increased water evaporation would take place, accompanied by copious global precipitation. In the aftermath, the dust and particulates in the atmosphere and stratosphere would screen out incoming infrared radiation from the sun. The warm ocean, in association with a cool atmosphere, would lead to precipitation as snow, hail and ice. Continental and polar ice sheets and alpine glaciers would expand. The result would be an ice age, or a succession of ice ages as conditions fluctuated.

Eventually, as the volcanic dust and debris settled out of the atmosphere under the influence of gravity, the atmosphere would warm up and ice would recede to its present positions.

A global giga-catastrophe on the scale indicated could produce all the features of the geologic column as a comparatively rapid succession of interrelated events. Strata would build up as various ecozones were destroyed and redeposited. Giant erosional features would result as the tsunamis receded from the land areas. Flood basalts and intrusive magmatic rocks would interpenetrate the developing land scenario. In the aftermath, a 'nuclear winter' type of climate would be expected until particulate settling from the atmosphere had progressed sufficiently far. This whole condition could develop from an earth movement not unlike that at Tōhoku but on a much larger scale. Overall, the 'gaps' in the geologic column would be eliminated and the geologic timescale would be downsized to thousands of years. A detailed interpretation of world geology, that matches this giga-catastrophe quite well, and describes it in terms of observed six megasequences, has recently been proposed by Timothy Clarey.[22] The Reference Chart on page xxii, comparing Deep Time with Compact Time, illustrates the dramatic transformation of the geologic column that would result.

Chapter 3: References and Notes

1. See W. Dembski and J. Wells, *How to Be an Intellectually Fulfilled Atheist (Or Not)*, Discovery Institute Press, Seattle, 2008.
2. See for example J. H. Shea, 'Twelve fallacies of uniformitarianism' in *Geology*, 1982, *10*, pp. 455–60; J. H. Shea, 'Editorial: Uniformitarianism and sedimentology' in *Journal of Sedimentary Petrology*, 1982, *52*, pp. 701–2.
3. U. B. Marvin, 'Impact and its revolutionary implications for geology' in *Global Catastrophes in Earth History: An Interdisciplinary Conference on Impacts, Volcanism and Mass Mortality*, V. L. Sharpton and D. Ward (eds.), Geological Society of America Special Paper, 1990, *247*, pp. 147–54.
4. D. V. Ager, *The Nature of the Stratigraphical Record*, Macmillan, London, 1973.
5. D. V. Ager, *The New Catastrophism: The Importance of the Rare Event in Geological History*, Cambridge University Press, Cambridge, 1993.
6. A. A. Snelling, *Earth's Catastrophic Past*, Volume 2, Institute of Creation Research, Dallas, 2009, pp. 477–610.
7. E. G. Nisbet and D. J. W. Piper, 'Ocean science: Giant submarine landslides' in *Nature*, 1998, *392*, pp. 329–30.
8. R. G. Rothwell, M. S. Reeder, G. Anastasakis, D. A. V. Stow, J. Thomson and G. Kähler, 'Low sea-level stand emplacement megaturbidites in the western and eastern Mediterranean Sea' in *Sedimentary Geology*, 2000, *135*, pp. 75–88.
9. B. F. Atwater and E. Hemphill-Haley, 'Recurrence intervals for great earthquakes of the past 3,500 years at northeastern Willapa Bay, Washington' in *US Geological Survey Professional Paper* 1,576, Reston, Virginia, US Geological Survey, 1997, p. 108.
10. E. G. Nisbet and D. J. W. Piper, 'Ocean science: Giant submarine landslides' in *Nature*, 1998, *392*, pp. 329–30.
11. S. Gupta, J. S. Collier, A. Palmer-Felgate and G. Potter, 'Catastrophic flooding origin of shelf valley systems in the English Channel' in *Nature*, 2007, 448 (7,151), pp. 342–5.
12. D. M. Raup and J. J. Sepkoski Jr., 'Mass extinctions in the marine fossil record' in *Science*, 1982, *215*, pp. 1,501–3.

13. (a) M. Allaby and J. Lovelock, *The Great Extinction*, Secker & Warburg, London, 1983; (b) D. M. Raup, *The Nemesis Affair*, Norton, New York and London, 1986; (c) C. C. Albritton Jr., *Catastrophic Episodes in Earth History*, Chapman & Hall, London, 1989.
14. (a) S. K. Donovan (ed.), *Mass Extinctions: Processes and Evidence*, Belhaven Press, London, 1989; (b) V. L. Sharpton and P. D. Ward (eds.), *Global Catastrophes in Earth History*, Geological Society of America Special Paper 247, 1990; (c) G. R. McGhee, *The Late Devonian Mass Extinction: The Frasnian/Famennian Crisis*, Columbia University Press, New York, 1996; (d) A. Hallam and P. B. Wignall, *Mass Extinctions and Their Aftermath*, Oxford University Press, Oxford, 1997.
15. T. Palmer, *Controversy, Catastrophism and Evolution: the Ongoing Debate*, Kluwer Academic/Plenum, New York, 1999.
16. M. R. Rampino and R. B. Stothers, 'Flood basalt volcanism during the past 250 million years' in *Science*, 1988, *241*, pp. 663–8.
17. J. S. Monroe and R. Wicander, *Physical Geology*, West Publishing, New York, 1992.
18. A. A. Snelling, *Earth's Catastrophic Past*, Volume 2, Ch. 69, pp. 537–47.
19. D. V. Ager, *The New Catastrophism: The Importance of the Rare Event in Geological History*, Cambridge University Press, Cambridge, 1993, pp. 197–8.
20. D. V. Ager, ibid., 1993, p. 14.
21. A. A. Snelling, *Earth's Catastrophic Past*, Volume 2, Ch. 62, p. 486.
22. T. Clarey, *Carved in Stone, Geological Evidence of the Worldwide Flood*, ICR, Dallas, 2020.

CHAPTER 4

FOOTPRINTS OF THE GIGA-CATASTROPHE

> *Study the past if you would define the future.*
> CONFUCIUS

> *The more you know about the past,*
> *the better prepared you are for the future.*
> THEODORE ROOSEVELT

FLOOD NARRATIVES FROM EVERY CONTINENT

The radiocarbon age data of fossil woods, shells and bones implies that the giga-catastrophe outlined in the previous chapter must have taken place thousands, not millions, of years ago. After such a comparatively short time it would be expected that vestiges of this unique, world-shaking event would be retained in the histories and folklore of people groups. It's highly significant to find, therefore, that narratives of a massive inundation feature prominently in folk history from all around the world. Anthropologists have consistently reported a group of legends that is common to practically every civilisation and culture. Hundreds of these, from different continents and geographical locations, tell of a huge, catastrophic flood that destroyed most of mankind, and that was survived by only a few individuals and animals.[1]

Flood legends have been reported from Babylon, Egypt, Sudan, Syria, Persia, India, China, Indonesia, Norway, Wales, Ireland, Romania, Mexico and many other places. A global motif is prominent in these flood legends. It is found in ancient Mesopotamian flood accounts, in Greek mythology with Deucalion and Pyrrha, in the Hebrew Genesis flood narrative, in the Lac Courte Oreilles Ojibwa Native American folk tales from North America, in oral traditions of Maasai, Yoruba and other African peoples, and in the traditional tales of some aboriginal tribes in Australia.[2]

In the Norse mythological *Prose Edda* of Snorri Sturluson, the proto-being Ymir was killed by Odin and his brothers. An enormous flood of blood flowed from Ymir's wounds. The only survivors were Bergelmir and his wife who escaped on a floating object. They later became the forebears of a new race called the *Jötunn*.

Anthropologists go so far as to say that the story of a great flood, and the brave attempts of human characters to control it, is fundamental to Chinese culture. It is key to understanding the origins of both the Xia and Zhou dynasties, and it is a major source of allusion in classical Chinese poetry. Traditionally, it is dated to about 2,300–2,200 BC.

There are several differing Greek flood legends. In Plato's *Timaeus*, written about 360 BC, the Bronze Race of humans angered the high god Zeus with their constant warring. Zeus decided to punish humanity with a flood. The Titan Prometheus, who had created humans from clay, told the secret plan to Deucalion, advising him to build an ark in order to be saved. After nine nights and days, the water started receding and the ark landed on a mountain. Plato argued that this flood had occurred about 10,000 BC.[3]

In an Indian flood legend, Manu was warned of an impending catastrophic flood by Matsya, the incarnation of Lord Vishnu as a fish. He was ordered to collect all the grains of the world in a boat. In some forms of the story, all living creatures were also to be preserved in the boat. The flood destroyed the world but Manu, in some versions accompanied by seven sages, survived by boarding the boat, which Matsya pulled to safety.[4]

The Sumerian flood story is probably the oldest on record. It was found on a broken cuneiform tablet dated to the 17th century BC. The council of gods decided to bring disaster upon mankind. The god Enki, speaking from behind a wall (indicative of a vision), informed Ziusudra of this and advised him to build a big boat. The flood lasted seven days and seven nights, after which Ziusudra left the boat and offered sacrifices to the gods. This story is thought to be the basis of similar legends found in the Babylonian Atrahasis and Gilgamesh epics. A tablet dated to about 1,635 BC relates that the gods decided to reduce the human population. Enki warned the hero Atrahasis to dismantle his house and build a boat to escape the flood planned by Enlil to destroy mankind. The boat was to have a roof, upper and lower decks, and to be sealed with bitumen. Atrahasis boarded the boat with his family and animals and sealed the door. The storm and flood were so huge even the gods were afraid. After seven days the flood ended and Atrahasis offered sacrifices to the gods. The *Epic of Gilgamesh* was first found on tablets from the 7th century BC. The hero-king Gilgamesh, who may have reigned somewhere in Sumer around 2,700 BC, journeyed to meet flood survivor Utnapishtim, who told him a detailed flood story very similar to that of Atrahasis.

Writing originated with the Sumerians in southern Mesopotamia probably around 3,000 BC. It is clear from ancient clay tablets that have survived from several Sumerian city states that these ancient peoples took for granted that the flood was a universal and momentous historical event. Their epic literature makes mention of it in several different contexts. Significantly, more than six versions of the *Sumerian King List*, or fragments thereof, have been unearthed and dated to as early as 2,000 BC. These lists, deriving from the first literate people, closest in time to the actual event, all divide the kings into antediluvian (pre-flood) and postdiluvian groups.

Several colourful flood stories have been collected in South America. In an Aztec account of a worldwide flood, two people, the hero Coxcox and his wife, survived the flood by floating in a boat that came to rest on a mountain. In the Toltec story a deluge destroyed the "first world" 1,716 years after it was created. Only a few people escaped this flood in a "closed chest". Robert Schoch mentions another ancient tribe of Mexico who told the story of a man named Tezpi who escaped the deluge in a boat filled with animals. "Tezpi released a vulture, which stayed away, gorging on cadavers. Then he let a hummingbird go, and it returned to him bearing a twig."[4]

The most detailed and rational account of the flood is the Hebrew one in Genesis.[5] First, God warned Noah and gave him enough time to build a boat or ark big enough to contain a representative sample of animals. Noah, his wife, their three sons, their wives, and the representative animals entered the ark. All the "springs of the great deep burst forth" and the floodgates of the heavens were opened. Rain fell on the Earth for forty days and forty nights, and water flooded the Earth for 150 days. All the high mountains under the entire heavens were covered. All land creatures not in the ark died. A great wind blew. Noah sent out bird scouts to test for dry land. The ark landed on the mountains of Ararat, was opened, and Noah made a thanksgiving sacrifice. Deriving chronological data from the Genesis narrative is fraught with difficulty, but a date for the flood not too different from 5,000 BP is indicated.[6]

The wide geographical distribution of flood legends is illustrated with some of the more than 270 known in Figure 4.1.

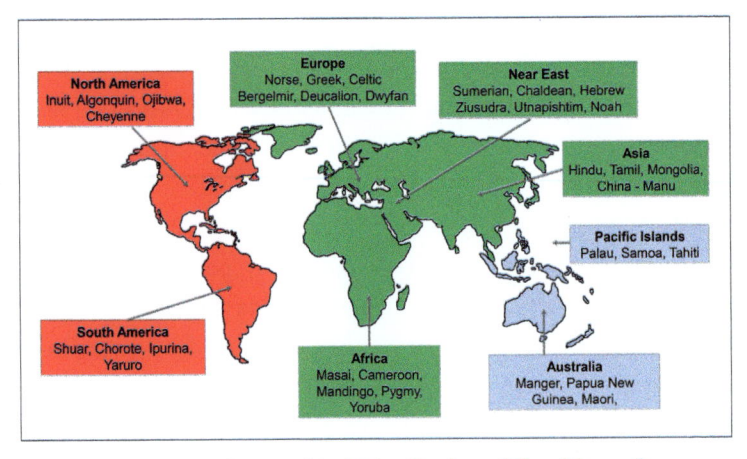

Figure 4.1: *Geographical Distribution of Flood Legends.*

In 95% of more than two hundred flood legends, the flood was worldwide; in 88%, a certain family was favoured; in 70%, survival was by means of a boat; in 67%, animals were also saved; in 66%, the flood was due to the wickedness of man; in 66%, the survivors had been forewarned; in 57%, they ended up on a mountain; in 35%, birds were sent out from the boat; and in 9%, exactly eight people were spared.[7] Figure 4.2 illustrates the remarkable number of elements these flood narratives have in common; remarkable because of the huge differences in country, culture, age and language of their sources.

Many of these stories originate from different historical epochs and civilisations that could not possibly have copied from one another. They derive from written and oral traditions dating from long before any missionaries arrived with the Genesis account of Noah. The natural conclusion to be drawn from so many congruent narratives is that in the distant past, there was a global flood that forever affected the history of all civilisations. These traditions agree in so many vital points it's most likely they originate from the same factual event.[8]

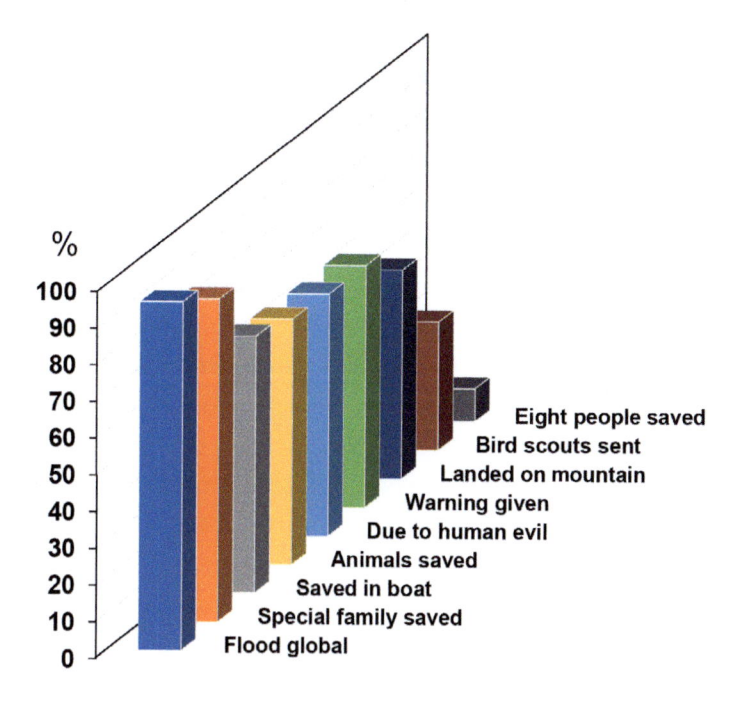

```
%
100
 90
 80
 70                                    Eight people saved
 60                                    Bird scouts sent
 50                                    Landed on mountain
 40                                    Warning given
                                       Due to human evil
 30                                    Animals saved
 20                                    Saved in boat
 10                                    Special family saved
  0                                    Flood global
```

Figure 4.2: *Common Elements in Two Hundred Flood Legends.*

Anthropologists maintain that a myth is often the faded memory of a real event. Details may have been added, lost, or obscured in the telling and retelling, but the kernel of truth remains. When two separate cultures have the same 'myth' in their body of folklore, their ancestors must have either experienced the same event, or they descended from a common ancestral source which itself experienced the event. It is undeniable that archaeological discoveries over more than a hundred years have generated a lot of respect for the historicity of ancient traditions, whether classical or biblical.

Critics maintain that all these accounts refer to local floods. This carries no conviction. Local floods are common; they come and go; they are familiar to everyone. They are particularly prevalent in Mesopotamia, where the Euphrates and Tigris Rivers flood often. There is no rationale for making one of them into a momentous, luminous ancestral tale. What is more, the language used in much of the folklore precludes local floods. If mountains were covered by the floodwater then it was not a local flood! It was far too deep and large. Only an enormous flood could float a boat the size of Noah's ark and land it on a mountain. Modern Mount Ararat is more than sixteen thousand feet (over five thousand metres) high! More than just a few people always survive local floods. There would be no point in building a boat to escape a local flood. Far easier to simply migrate to the nearest high ground! Again, there would be no need to take animals on board a ship to avoid a local flood. They could safely and simply escape or be herded out of reach of the water. The Genesis text mentions birds more than any other creatures. Many other flood accounts also mention birds. If the flood wasn't totally global then it would be completely unnecessary to take birds into the ark. They could easily fly to any areas not covered by water and rest there. Only in a truly global flood would birds have nowhere to land and rest. [8]

The soundest way to understand the widespread, similar flood legends is to recognise their kernel of authenticity. All the world's peoples, though separated geographically, linguistically and culturally, have descended from a group of real survivors of a real global flood. They survived on a real boat which eventually landed on a real mountain. The survival drama of this apocalyptic event has never been forgotten.

When Did the Giga-Catastrophe Take Place?

The flood narratives readily correlate with the giga-catastrophe outlined in Chapter 3. The front-line encounter of the human population with the giga-catastrophe would have been with tsunami waves sweeping inland, and the accompanying precipitation. It would be perceived as a flood, and it would be a flood that would have to be survived.

All the then-existing biosphere would have been buried during episodic events of the giga-catastrophe. Land and sea creatures, plus all plants, trees and vegetation, would have been submerged, compressed and transmuted into the carbon-containing strata observed today. It's well established that coal, oil and natural gas can all form rapidly under suitable conditions and in the presence of appropriate clay, mineral and bacterial catalysts.[9,10] The copious shale and carbonate rocks can be attributed to the same event. A huge amount of carbon would have been removed from the active biosphere during the short duration of the disaster.

The giga-catastrophe would certainly have brought about the extinction of many types of flora and fauna. More extinctions would follow because of the destruction of habitats crucial to individual species. However, once the initiating high-energy processes had run their course and the waters had receded from the land, plant life would rapidly start to reappear. It's of interest to assess the longevity of living plants and vegetation stretching back in time towards the giga-catastrophe. Enormous radiometric ages have been attributed to certain clonal plant and fungal colonies; but these need to be viewed with a strong dose of scepticism.

Trees are certainly the longest-living organisms, and can be dated independently of radiometric methods by counting their annual growth rings. Several varieties of trees are known to have been living for thousands of years. Figure 4.3 displays the ages of the oldest trees according to ring counts. The giant sequoias in Sequoia National Park, California, live to great ages, and trees up to about 3,200 years old are known. The Llangernyw Yew, located in the churchyard of the village of Llangernyw in North Wales, is believed to be aged between four thousand and five thousand years.

The bristlecone pines found in the higher mountains of California, Nevada and Utah are the oldest living individual trees.[11] 'Methuselah', one such pine in a grove of about ten, was given an age of 4,851 years from its ring count, and was long reckoned to be the world's oldest living organism.

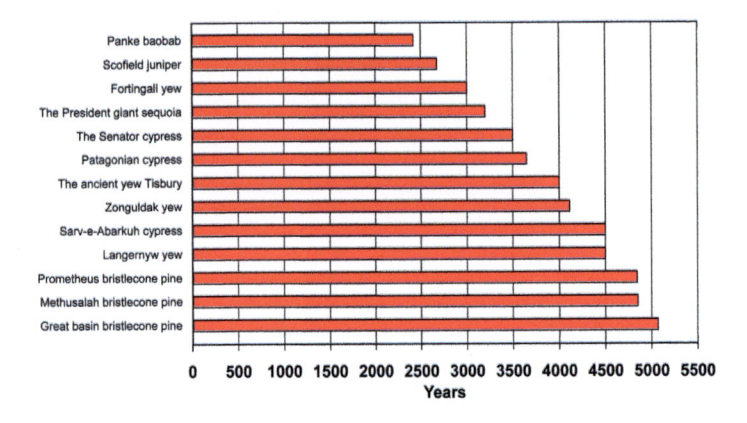

Figure 4.3: *Age Spread of the World's Most Ancient Trees.*

These bristlecone pines certainly have the appearance of great age, as Figure 4.4 shows. Recently, an older bristlecone pine has been discovered in the White Mountains of California and its ring count indicates an age of 5,069 years. This is the longest lifespan of any single living organism, stretching from the present back towards the time of the giga-catastrophe.

Figure 4.4: *Bristlecone Pine, White Mountains, California.*
Photo courtesy of Dr Tim Standish.

By assuming these bristlecone pines started to grow immediately after the giga-catastrophe, a date for it of somewhat older than 5,000 BP can be arrived at. This date is in rough accord with the times of the global flood derived from the Chinese, Hebrew and Babylonian flood narratives.

Chapter 4: References and Notes

1. See for example A. M. Rehwinkel, *The Flood*, St. Louis, Missouri, Concordia, 1951.
2. J. Perloff, *Tornado in a Junkyard: The Relentless Myth of Darwinism*, Refuge Books, Arlington, Massachusetts, 1999.
3. Plato's Timaeus. Greek text: http://www.24grammata.com/wp-content/uploads/2011/01/Platon-Timaios.pdf
4. R. M. Schoch, *Voyages of the Pyramid Builders*, Jeremy P. Tarcher, Putnam, New York, 2003.
5. Genesis, Chs. 6–8.
6. See (a) U. Cassuto, *A Commentary on the Book of Genesis: From Adam to Noah*, 1961, Magnes Press, Jerusalem; (b) G. F. Hasel, 'The meaning of the chronogenealogies of Genesis 5 and 11' in *Origins*, 1980, 7(2), pp. 53–70; (c) P. J. Ray Jr., 'An evaluation of the numerical variants of the chronogenealogies of Genesis 5 and 11' in *Origins*, 1985, 12(1), 26–37.
7. B. C. Nelson, 'Appendix 11: Flood Traditions' in *The Deluge Story in Stone*, Augsburg, Minneapolis, 1931; see Figure 38.
8. For a detailed feasibility study of the survival of representatives of human and animal life on a boat during the great flood, see J. Woodmorappe, *Noah's Ark: A Feasibility Study*, Institute of Creation Research, 1996.
9. R. Hayatsu, R. L. McBeth, R. G. Scott, R. E. Botto and R. E. Winans, 'Artificial coalification study: preparation and characterization of synthetic macerals' in *Organic Geochemistry*, 1984, 6, pp. 463–71.
10. A. A. Snelling and J. B. Mackay, 'Evidence of catastrophic deposition of coals and sediments of the Newcastle coal measures' in *Proceedings of the Nineteenth Symposium on Advances in the Study of the Sydney Basin*, Department of Geology, University of Newcastle, New South Wales, 1985, pp. 110–13; A. A. Snelling and J. B. Mackay, 'The role of volcanism in the rapid formation of coal seams: The Walloon Coal Measures of Queensland and New South Wales – a case study' in *Proceedings of the 1985 International Conference on Coal Science*, Pergamon Press, Sydney, 1985, p. 641.
11. G. Moore, B. Kershner, T. Craig, M. Daniel, G. Nelson; R. Spellenberg, J. W. Thieret, P. Terry and A. Block, *National*

Wildlife Federation Field Guide to Trees of North America, Sterling, New York, 2008, p. 82.

Chapter 5

A Carbon Clock For Compact Time

> *I regard consensus science as an extremely pernicious development that ought to be stopped cold in its tracks. Historically, the claim of consensus has been the first refuge of scoundrels; it is a way to avoid debate by claiming that the matter is already settled... Consensus is the business of politics. Science, on the contrary... has results that are verifiable by reference to the real world... What are relevant are reproducible results. The greatest scientists in history are great precisely because they broke with the consensus. There is no such thing as consensus science. If it's consensus, it isn't science. If it's science, it isn't consensus. Period.*
>
> Michael Crichton

> *Education is the ability to listen to almost anything without losing your temper.*
>
> Robert Frost

Large-Scale Burial of Carbon

A timing method is needed to enable an Earth chronology based around Compact Time to be constructed. A clock based on experimental field data is required that will disclose the real ages of rocks, fossils and artefacts. Radiocarbon provides a valuable and promising body of data. The huge perturbation to the atmospheric level of ^{14}C caused by the giga-catastrophe must be factored into the evaluation of the raw quantities of ^{14}C obtained by AMS analysis of rock samples. The geologic column contains enormous amounts of carbon-containing rocks and minerals. Since all of this was deposited in a short time during the giga-catastrophe, the biosphere prior to this was much larger and more luxuriant than at present. Several scientists have made estimates of the total of this buried carbon, leading to the conclusion that the biosphere prior to the giga-catastrophe had three to seven hundred times as much carbon as at present.[1–3] Inescapably, this finding has deep-seated implications for radiocarbon dating.

A reasonable initial assumption is that cosmic ray activity before the catastrophe was about the same as today, and therefore that the production rate of ^{14}C was also about the same. Take five hundred times the present as the assumed value for the relative size of the pre-catastrophe biosphere. Then, before the giga-catastrophe, the same quantity of ^{14}C as today was diluted amongst five hundred times as much total carbon. The $^{14}C/C$ ratio would be one five-hundredth of its present size, or about 0.2 in terms of pMC. Of course, this is a rough estimate and a 'soft' number. The assumption in conventional radiocarbon dating is that the $^{14}C/C$ ratio, measured in a fossil, is the residue after decay from (roughly) the present atmospheric $^{14}C/C$ ratio. If, however, the original $^{14}C/C$ ratio was only one five-hundredth of this, then the 'true' radiocarbon age of the fossil would be dramatically less.

What is more, other factors will, of course, impact on the situation. The cosmic ray intensity is known to depend on sunspot activity and other processes in the sun's photosphere. The Earth's magnetic field deflects cosmic rays away from the Earth's atmosphere. The direction and intensity of the magnetic field have been observed to change over time. During the last two centuries, the dipole strength has been decreasing at a rate of about 6.3% per century.[4] If this were the continuation of monotonic decay from the past, the field would have been much greater five thousand years ago and this would have further reduced the ^{14}C/C ratio in the pre-catastrophic atmosphere. Long extrapolations such as this are seldom safe, and actually numerous complete reversals of the field are indicated by palaeomagnetic data.

Several scientists have devised means of calibrating radiocarbon data to factor in the increase in atmospheric carbon-14 after the flood.[5-7] The most interesting and applicable method was devised by physicist Robert H. Brown. After his PhD studies at the University of Washington, Brown did research on proximity-fused artillery, radar and secure radio communication during World War II. He also worked for the US Naval Radiological Defense Laboratory on a precursor to sonar. Brown became interested in radioactivity and trained in radioisotope techniques at the Oak Ridge Institute of Nuclear Studies. Following this, he carried through a comprehensive series of investigations into ^{14}C dating. He examined radiocarbon dating of peat bogs, of lake sediments, of cave deposits and of other sedimentary layers in relation to their depth. These age/depth profiles convinced him that the ^{14}C/C ratio had been less in the past. He also studied the amino acid dating technique in relation to radiocarbon dating and found corroborating evidence. He decided that a quantitative method for converting radiocarbon data to real time, taking into account the past global catastrophe, ought to be and could be developed.

Quantitative Model for ¹⁴C Evolution after the Giga-Catastrophe

Brown assumed that the $^{14}C/C$ level increased rapidly and exponentially after the giga-catastrophe to its present level over a few hundred years. That this rapid increase was a reasonable assumption was shown by the rapid 90% rise in the $^{14}C/C$ level as atomic bomb testing proceeded, and then the equally rapid decline during the 1980s and '90s.[8] Figure 5.1 illustrates the form of the function that models the idea behind this assumption. The $^{14}C/C$ ratio started at about 0.2 pMC sometime before about 5,000 BP. As the vast quantities of carbon were removed from the biosphere and buried during the giga-catastrophe, the $^{14}C/C$ ratio would rise dramatically and exponentially to its present level.

Brown made the assumption that the net effect of all factors contributing to the evolving increase of the $^{14}C/C$ level could be represented by a single exponential function. He deduced reasonable estimates of the parameters in this function from the known good correspondence between ^{14}C ages and real-time historical ages from the present to about 3,500 BP. His radiocarbon calibration method appears in a series of papers,[1,9-12] and the relationship he obtained is shown as Equation (1):

$$\exp(-T_{14}/8,300) = \exp[-T_M/8,300]\{1-\exp[-\alpha(D_C-T_M)]\} \qquad (1)$$

Here, T_{14} is the uncorrected radiocarbon age, 8,300 years is the mean radiocarbon life (half-life of 5,730 divided by $\ln(2)$ and rounded), T_M is the carbon Compact Time (CpT) model age, α is a parameter that controls the exponential rate at which the $^{14}C/C$ ratio rises to its post-catastrophe value, and D_C is the date of the giga-catastrophe.

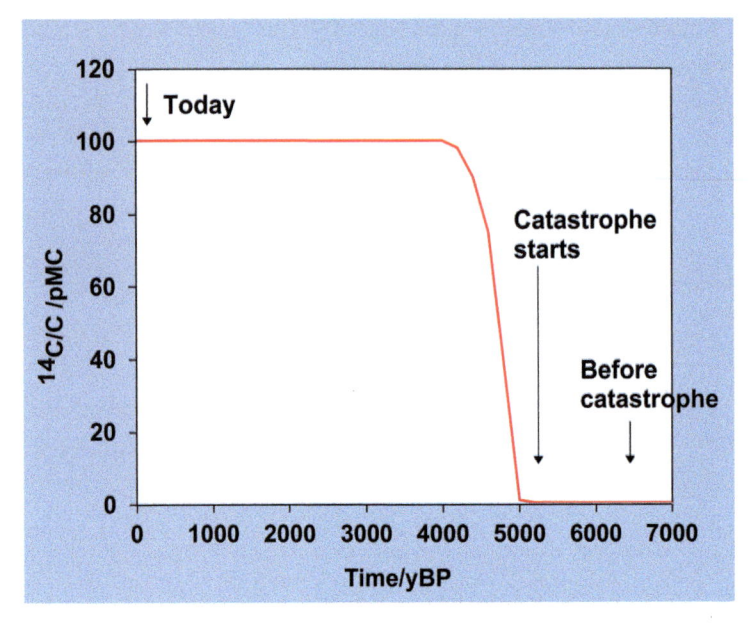

[Figure: graph of ¹⁴C/C ratio vs Time/yBP, with axis 0–120 pMC, showing "Today" at left, flat near 100 pMC until ~5000 BP, then steep drop labeled "Catastrophe starts" and "Before catastrophe" near 0 pMC beyond ~5500 BP.]

Figure 5.1: *Time Profile of the ¹⁴C/C Ratio Before, During and After the Giga-Catastrophe.*

Alternatively, this can be written as:

$$T_M = T_{14} + 8{,}300\{\ln[1-\exp(-\alpha(D_C - T_{14}))/1{,}000]^{-1}\} \qquad (2)$$

Equations (1) and (2) provide an approximate mathematical relationship that models a smooth transition of the upper biosphere ¹⁴C/C ratio from about 1 pMC to 95 pMC during four thousand real-time years. It can readily be adapted for different dates for the giga-catastrophe and for different biosphere ¹⁴C levels at that time. Brown deduced a value of $\alpha = 3.0$ by assuming the ¹⁴C/C ratio rose from about 0.1 pMC at 5,000 BP to its present level at 4,000 BP. For an assumed date for the giga-catastrophe of $D_C = 5{,}350$ BP, a value of $\alpha = 3.2$ is most appropriate.[13] These expressions are only valid from the time of the giga-catastrophe

¹⁴C in Fossil pMC	Conventional ¹⁴C Date (BP, T_{14})	Compact Time ¹⁴C Date (BP, T_M)
100	0	0
88.6	1,000	1,000
78.5	2,000	2,000
73.9	2,501	2,500
69.5	3,005	3,000
66.2	3,416	3,400
62.7	3,858	3,800
60.8	4,111	4,000
58.6	4,412	4,200
55.9	4,807	4,400
52.1	5,389	4,600
49.5	5,808	4,700
46.3	6,367	4,800
42.1	7,144	4,900
36.7	8,278	5,000
29.6	10,052	5,100
25.3	11,369	5,150
20.2	13,204	5,200
14.4	16,000	5,250
7.73	21,166	5,300
6.27	22,898	5,310
4.76	25,166	5,320
3.22	28,410	5,330
1.63	34,041	5,340
0.8	39,900	5,345
0.4	45,600	5,350
0.2	51,400	5,350
0.1	57,100	5,350

Table 5.1: *Conversion Table for Radiocarbon Data.*

to the present. No information is currently available about the evolution of the $^{14}C/C$ ratio before the global catastrophe.

Table 5.1 contains a list of the conventional, uncalibrated ^{14}C dates corresponding to the amounts of radiocarbon (in pMC) measured in specimens. The corresponding Compact Time model dates, calculated from Equation (2) with these assumptions, are displayed alongside in the third column. A plot of the CpT model ages vs. uncalibrated radiocarbon ages, calculated from Equation (2), appears in Figure 5.2.

In Figure 5.2 the published, conventional, uncalibrated ^{14}C ages (T_{14}) are plotted along the horizontal axis. The corresponding CpT model ages (T_M), from Equation (2) are on the vertical axis. The full curved line corresponds to the age calibration with the CpT model. For comparison, the straight dotted line indicates how uncalibrated ^{14}C ages, ignoring the giga-catastrophe, develop linearly over the same time interval.

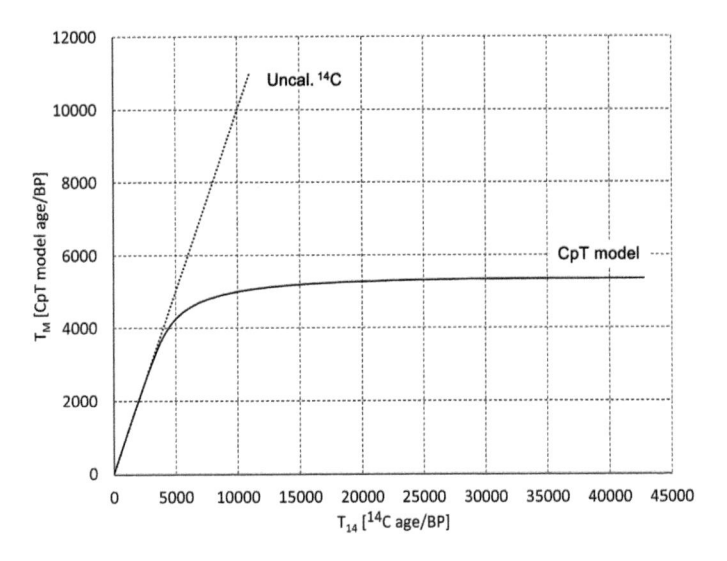

Figure 5.2: *Effect of the Giga-Catastrophe on Radiocarbon Dates – the CpT Model Ages.*

The CpT model ages increase linearly from the present to about 3,500 BP, then start to level off. For radiocarbon ages (T_{14}) of beyond about 10,000 BP, the CpT model ages approach T_M ~5,350 BP roughly asymptotically. Note that the CpT model ages, and the uncalibrated radiocarbon ages, are in good agreement with one another till 3,000–3,500 BP (1,000–1,500 BC). The model predicts that published radiocarbon dates from historical periods back till then should be reliable and will agree with archaeo-historical data, exactly as is found in practice. Further back in time the two lines diverge, such that the CpT model yields younger dates than the uncalibrated ^{14}C dates. The difference gets greater the older the samples are. Authentic ages of fossils and artefacts, allowing for the giga-catastrophe, can be obtained by using this CpT model relationship to correct reported ^{14}C dates.

Historical Perspective on Radiocarbon Dating of Bronze Age Materials

The first prediction of the CpT model is, therefore, that reported ^{14}C dates for specimens, artefacts and events from earlier than about 1,000–1,500 BC will be *older* than the dates obtained by independent historical and archaeological methods. Moreover, the older a specimen is, the greater will be this trend towards older conventional ^{14}C dates. This offers excellent means of testing the CpT model. These predictions should be testable from independent published data by comparisons of the ^{14}C dates with archaeo-historical dates (A/H dates) when both have been obtained for the same specimen or event.

The most reliable historical chronologies are those of Mesopotamia, Egypt and the Near East. These have been developed by archaeologists and historians over many decades from meticulous and painstaking comparisons of stratigraphy, pottery, artefacts, writings, inscribed tablets, king lists, ostraca, astronomical data, and monuments obtained from securely dated sites. From about 1,000 BC to the present, radiocarbon age data for these civilisations agrees well with A/H chronologies. For earlier eras in the Bronze Age and before, serious difficulties in reconciling ^{14}C data with historical data have been widely reported.[14-16] The problems created by radiocarbon dating in Mesopotamian and Egyptian chronologies were comprehensively reviewed by Michael Hasel.[17] The apparently irreconcilable conflicts were also clearly set out by David Rohl.[18]

The finding of conventional radiocarbon dates from Early, Middle and Late Bronze Age sites in the Middle and Near East (ca. 1,200–3,100 BC) that are older than historical dates (too high) is so common as to be nearly universal. Some selected example quotations will illustrate the extent of the problem. A wide-ranging comparison of ^{14}C dates with historical dates was published by James Mellaart.[19] Commenting on this, Hasel wrote:

> *Mellaart should be commended for his attempt to correlate the two apparently contradictory sources of information for the dating of early Mesopotamian periods. However, it seems apparent that this most recent attempt to reconcile the ^{14}C dating and historical chronology fails to provide any conclusive new evidence. The ^{14}C dates were consistently too high for even the "ultra-high" chronology which completely lacks support from the Venus data and archaeological stratification.[17]*

Bruins and van der Plicht reported that high-quality ^{14}C dates from Early Bronze Age Jericho are "100–300 years older than conventional archaeo-historical time estimates". Furthermore, they noted:

> *In conclusion, the collective ^{14}C evidence of the Early Bronze Age from Jericho and other sites in the southern Levant, as well as from Egypt for the Predynastic period and Dynasties 1–6, strongly challenges the current archaeo-historical time framework for these cultural and political periods. Most ^{14}C dates overwhelmingly show that these periods are significantly older than currently accepted.*[20]

Braun determined from another study that resulted in older ^{14}C dates that "the logical outcome of an acceptance of these new dates [from the southern Levant and Egypt] puts such a strain on chronological correlations between the ^{14}C data and the archaeological record, that the entire system would no longer be tenable if accepted".[21] Archaeologist Arthur Knapp wrote that ^{14}C dates "deviate increasingly from actual calendar dates: from a 200-year error around 1000 BC up to a 900-year error around 5000 BC".[22] Egyptologist H. Haas and colleagues obtained high-precision ^{14}C dates for Egyptian Old Kingdom items (ca. 2,200–2,600 BC), but reported that they were an average of 374 years older than historical dates given in *The Cambridge Ancient History*.[23] Eminent Israeli archaeologist Amihai Mazar is on record as refusing to use ^{14}C dating for Palestinian archaeology for remains from the 3rd and 4th millennia BC.[24]

In an interesting appendix to his book *A Test of Time*, Egyptologist David Rohl wrote:

> *...the difference between C-14 dates and historical dates from the third millennium BC and earlier is of such magnitude that historians cannot afford to view the matter this way. Similarly, the consequences of using C-14 dating to fix an absolute date for both the start and end of the 18th Dynasty (ca. 1550–1300 BC) are also unacceptable: the historian is required to find an extra*

> *120 years of Egyptian 'history' for which there is absolutely no archaeological evidence.*[18]

Rohl illustrated the scale of the problem by means of a chart in which the historical dates of events and of pharaohs' reigns were plotted against the calibrated ^{14}C dates. The chart shows the deviation of the ^{14}C dates progressively increasing from zero at about 1,200 BC to at least five hundred years by 2,700 BC. All these statements from specialists and experts agree well with the predictions from the CpT model and tend to validate it.

The dispute between radiocarbon chronologists and historians has been rumbling on for many decades, with mounting frustration at the inability to resolve the differences. Revised chronologies appear from time to time, have a short vogue and then go out of favour. One identified problem was that of 'old wood'. Timber incorporated into a temple might have been old timber reused from a previous building. The ^{14}C date would then be older, possibly by hundreds of years, than the date of construction of the temple or the age of its builders. However, this did not apply for short-life specimens of seeds, grains, charcoal or bones; yet the same discrepancy of older ^{14}C dates persisted with these materials. On one hand, radiocarbon chronologists uphold the scientific rigour of their 'high-precision' absolute dates. They point to the good concord of radiocarbon dates with historical dates for the period up to about 1,000 BC. They have repeatedly advocated either ultra-high chronologies for Near Eastern civilisations, or else a complete revision and drastic lengthening of Bronze Age chronologies.

On the other hand, archaeologists, and historians from their perspective, point to the 'empty centuries' that longer chronologies inevitably produce. Monarchs in the Near East could expect to reign on average for about ten to twenty years, so lengthening a dynasty by only one hundred years means finding at least five additional kings for whom there is absolutely no historical or archaeological evidence. In fact, archaeological and historical discoveries over the last sixty years have encouraged the opposite trend towards shorter chronologies of the Near East.[17] This is due to the recognition of many more co-regencies amongst the monarchs, and of instances of two kings reigning simultaneously over different parts of the same territory. Historians try to accommodate the ^{14}C data by positing high, medium and low chronologies, whilst making it clear that they favour the latter. They remain suspicious that there is 'something wrong' with ^{14}C dating for the era in question.

This long-standing, apparently irreconcilable conflict is symptomatic of a deep malaise affecting the current understanding of ancient earth history and prehistory. In fact, it points to the fundamental unsoundness of Deep Time. Although the radiocarbon method claims rigorous scientific credentials, it is only as good as its underlying assumptions. One of these is the uniformitarian-inspired extrapolation into the past of approximately the same ^{14}C level in the biosphere as at present. But the global giga-catastrophe invalidates this assumption. It is apparent that the 'something wrong' with radiocarbon dating is the failure to recognise the effect on the ^{14}C/C ratio in the biosphere of a massive global catastrophe not long before 5,000 BP. Radiocarbon chronologists have laboured over many years to calibrate the method for comparatively minor fluctuations in this ratio, principally by means of dendrochronology (see below on this method). Use of the more drastic calibration of ^{14}C dates, to include the huge disturbance resulting from the global giga-catastrophe, would go a long way towards reconciling the historical and radiocarbon chronologies of ancient Near Eastern civilisations.

Comparison of Conventional ^{14}C and CpT Model Dates with Archaeo-Historical Dates

The statements from expert chronologists and historians recorded above qualitatively confirm that the predictions from the Brown CpT model stand up well. A more quantitative assessment of the model would obviously be desirable. This is a non-trivial exercise for Bronze Age civilisations because the remoteness of the era stretches archaeo-historical chronological methods to the limit of their effectiveness. Then, too, radiocarbon dating has undergone numerous modifications and adjustments in the last decades. Early ^{14}C dates were uncalibrated and often obtained with less accurate counting equipment. Previously, a plethora of different calibration methods were applied as these techniques developed in the latter half of the 20th century. The result is that ^{14}C dates in the literature, particularly the older ones, are not always reliable or consistent with one another. Great care is needed, therefore, in assessing both types of dates.

An immense body of chronological data from Bronze Age civilisations is available in books and periodicals. A selection of this data, designed to give a cross section of new and old reports, crossing several diverse cultures and representing the standpoint of both radiometric chronologists and historians, was made. Most radiocarbon dates are now reported as calibrated dates that attempt to allow for minor variations in the biosphere ^{14}C/C ratio by means of dendrochronological science. The calibrations are non-linear and contain long-range and short-range fluctuations referred to as 'wiggles'. A consequence of the short-range wiggles is that a given ^{14}C result may yield a (small) group of calibrated dates. Where date groups have been reported, for convenience of plotting, the average of these was taken.

Bruins and van der Plicht obtained AMS and conventional radiocarbon dates for short-lived material from Early Bronze (EB)

Age phases at Jericho and found them to be significantly older than conventional archaeo-historical dates.[20] The mean values of the radiocarbon and historical dates they listed for transitions between the EB phases are plotted in Figure 5.3 as 'EBJer' with triangle symbols. In another article, they presented calibrated radiocarbon dates for successions of phases at Tell el-Dabᶜa and at Ashkelon.[25] The archaeo-historical date for the Minoan Santorini eruption was within the ^{14}C age range they obtained. However, most of their reported ^{14}C dates for different phases at these sites were again older than the historical dates. This data set is named 'MEast' with triangle symbols in Figure 5.3.

Regev and colleagues prepared an extensive summary and evaluation of radiocarbon dates for Early Bronze Age sites in the southern Levant including Jericho, Yarmuth and Tell el-Umeiri.[26] Their data for the transitions between the various EB Age phases appears in Figure 5.3 as 'EB1to4' with square symbols. Egyptologist David Rohl has advocated a revised chronology for Egypt, but he also presented conventional historical dates in his books.[18,27] A selection of these dates is plotted in Figure 5.3 as 'Egypt1' with circle symbols. A set of data for prominent monarchs, individuals and events was culled from various sources[18,28–30] and is plotted in Figure 5.3 as 'Misc', also with circle symbols.

James Mellaart assembled radiocarbon dates for several Near East civilisations as part of an effort to reconcile the archaeo-historical chronology of Egypt and Palestine with radiocarbon dates.[19] He proposed an ultra-high chronology for Egypt that historians deemed far too high.[31,32] Radiocarbon dates from Mellaart are plotted in Figure 5.3, with historical dates recommended by *The Cambridge Ancient History*'s third edition,[33] as 'Egypt2' (squares).

Virtually every specimen, from different radiocarbon dating laboratories, and from different Near and Middle Eastern

Bronze Age sites, yielded calibrated ^{14}C dates that were older than the archaeo-historical dates. It is very remarkable that such conspicuous dissonance between chronologies obtained by careful professional archaeologists and radio-chronologists has persisted for so long.

The seriousness of the disparity shows up clearly when the data is compared graphically. The sets of archaeo-historical ages (A/H-age) are graphed against their corresponding calibrated ^{14}C ages BP in Figure 5.3.

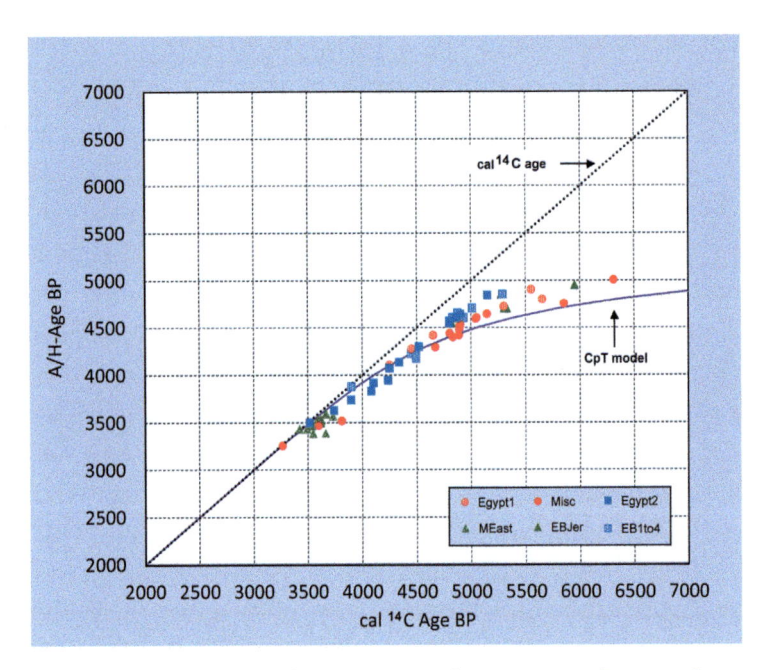

Figure 5.3: *Relationship Between Archaeo-Historical Ages and Calibrated ^{14}C Ages, Together with the CpT Model from Equation (2).*

It is not possible to derive realistic error limits on the individual data points; but these are certainly large. The age ranges quoted for many of the ^{14}C dates were of the order of one hundred years. The error limits of the younger archaeo-historical dates were comparatively small, but they increase substantially for the Early Bronze and Chalcolithic data. These uncertainties do not, however, obscure the overall trend, which is distinctly non-linear and levels off for the older specimens. For comparison, the dotted line indicates the linear relationship, with unit gradient, that would be obtained if the published ^{14}C ages had matched the independent archaeo-historical ages.

Figure 5.3 highlights the divergence between the A/H dates and the calibrated ^{14}C dates. The A/H dates are already around a hundred years younger than the cal^{14}C dates by 4,000 BP, and reach about a thousand years younger by 6,000 BP on the horizontal axis. This places into high relief the cause of the prevailing unease between radiocarbon and historical chronologists. The graphic also illustrates that the trend in the age observations is levelling out towards a limit somewhere between 5,000 and 5,500 BP on the vertical A/H-age axis.

The full line is a plot of the CpT model ages calculated from Equation (2) and assuming a date of 5,350 BP for the giga-catastrophe. The model matches the observational data remarkably well up to at least a cal^{14}C of 5,000 BP on the horizontal axis. The uncertainties are greater in the historical dates of specimens older than this; i.e. from the era of the first few dynasties in Egypt and before. The CpT model line probably lies within the error limits of the A/H observations. It would definitely be advantageous to extend the observations to earlier times in the Predynastic and Chalcolithic periods. Some data does exist for these times, but the contexts of historical sites this old are difficult to pinpoint, so A/H dates are not soundly based and are prone to being coloured by the 'high' dates afforded by the emerging torrent of radiocarbon determinations.

Certainly, the form of the relationship in Figure 5.3 provides strong support for the placement of the giga-catastrophe not long before 5,000 BP. The CpT model relationship, with minor modifications such as inclusion of the dendrochronological wiggles for dates younger than about 3,500 BP, could be used in place of the IntCal13 calibration curve[34] to calibrate raw ^{14}C data. This would promptly bring ^{14}C dates into conformity with archaeo-historical dates and bring about a happy resolution of the interdisciplinary conflict.

Radiocarbon Dating and Dendrochronology: An Intimate Relationship

It might be claimed that the accuracy of radiocarbon dating has been affirmed, validated and even enhanced by tree-ring dating back to before 10,000 BP. The two techniques exist, however, in a reciprocal, almost symbiotic relationship. From quite early on it was realised that radiocarbon dates were affected by variations in the atmospheric ^{14}C/C ratio. To correct for these fluctuations, recourse was had to master chronologies derived from other chronological information. For the period back to about 10,000 BP, tree-ring dating, also called dendrochronology, is the principal source of these data. Several separate master chronologies have been developed from painstaking studies of tree-ring width variations over time. Ring patterns were obtained from the remarkably long-lived bristlecone pines of California, from Irish oaks, from German oaks and from trees of other regions.

A variety of curves for calibrating ^{14}C dates were created and used in the second half of the 20th century. At present, the generally accepted calibration is IntCal13.[34] A calibration curve called Marine13, stretching back to about 50,000 BP, was developed for marine samples from coral specimens dated by both radiocarbon and ^{230}Th/^{238}U methods. Reasons for serious scepticism about the results from radiometric methods like $^{230}Th/^{238}U$ were presented in Chapter 1. It should also be noted that the percentages of ^{14}C, measured in corals allegedly 20,000–50,000 BP, are *in the same range* as the ^{14}C percentages measured for coal samples allegedly 300 Ma and dinosaur fossils allegedly 66 Ma. These small amounts of ^{14}C are routinely dismissed as 'contamination' in coal samples. It is obviously unacceptable practice to discount data in one context – that is, the pre-Pleistocene era – but treat the same data as valid for chronological purposes in another. Accepting that the ^{14}C levels determined for the coral samples are valid, the ages attributed to them will nevertheless be grossly inflated. That's because the real-time relationship, developed from archaeo-historical data dips well below the ^{14}C age conversion line, as Figure 5.3 demonstrates. The CpT model yields ages for the corals that are tens of thousands of years younger than alleged. In short, the Marine13 calibration should be viewed with healthy scepticism.

Various features of the IntCal13 calibration back to about 10,000 BP, as illustrated in Figure 5.4, are noteworthy. The calibrated dates are older than the uncalibrated ones. The calibration curve exhibits a long-term sinusoidal feature together with short-term modulations, the 'wiggles', that are irregular and typically extend over tens of years. The raw AMS ^{14}C analytical data for a fossil forms a normal bell-shaped distribution of dates. On comparing this with the IntCal13 calibration curve, the wiggles enable a range of possible calibrated dates with several optimum values to be specified.[35]

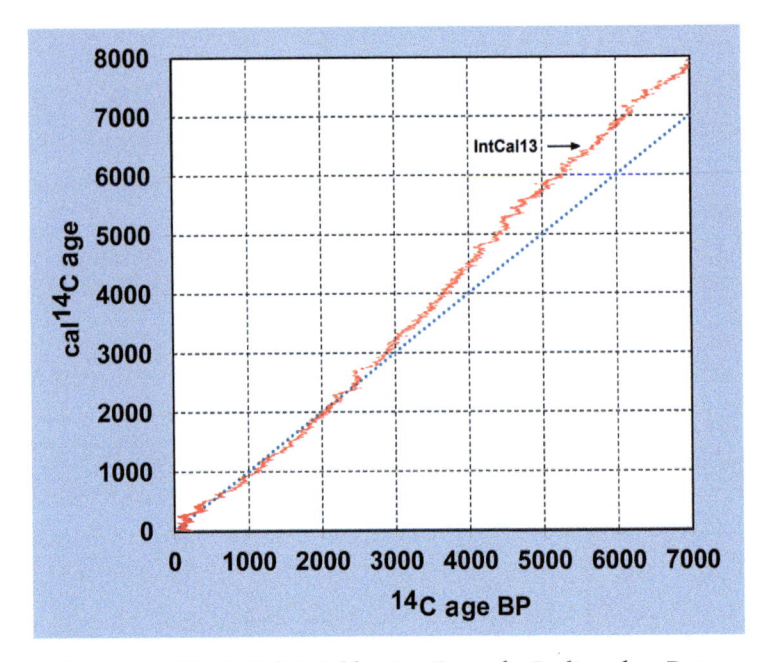

Figure 5.4: *The IntCal13 Calibration Curve for Radiocarbon Dates.*

Tree-ring patterns are obtained from tree cores, from cross sections, or otherwise, and the widths of the rings are measured either by hand or from digitised scans. Figure 5.5 shows a cross section through an ancient bristlecone pine with an expanded view of a section of the rings. Some idea of the difficulty of achieving definitive values of the widths of individual rings can be obtained from examining this.

Diagrams of ring widths plotted against ring numbers, usually like those shown in Figure 5.6, are then produced. The ring widths depend on climatic conditions including the atmospheric CO_2 level. For living trees, the dates of each ring can be ascertained, independent of ^{14}C dating, by simply counting from the outermost ring inwards to the tree centre. Simultaneously, individual rings can be ^{14}C dated, and hence a

Figure 5.5: *Cross Sections Through a 3,046-Year-Old Great Basin Bristlecone Pine.*
Photos courtesy of Dr Tim Standish.

plot of the tree-ring date against the ^{14}C date gives a very valid way of calibrating the latter for climatic fluctuations of ^{14}C levels.

Extending these calibrations back in time, beyond the lifetime of living trees, requires stumps and logs of dead trees, including those buried in bogs and other sediments, to be employed. Chronological data for these trees can be derived from ring width data, but the age at which the tree was felled or died is not known. The date of the first ring must be estimated by some other means. Ideally, the ring pattern of the dead tree is compared with the pattern of the master chronology of known age by means of sophisticated statistical methods. From the statistical best fit, the overlapping part of the pattern from the dead tree can be matched to part of the master chronology pattern. For older dead trees this enables the master chronology to be extended further back in time. This process often works well, such that the master chronologies extending back a few thousand years can be regarded as sound.

Frequently, however, the statistical comparison of the dead tree pattern with the master chronology gives several, or even many, fits with correlation parameters (t-test values) indicating high probability. Figure 5.5 shows the complexity and irregularity the width patterns often display. So, for example, for dead Tree X a cross-match 1 to the master chronology with a t-test value >3.2, implying high probability, may be found as one amongst several matches. Radiocarbon dating of the dead tree will be consulted to decide which match to accept. If the radiocarbon date is compatible, then Match 1, which extends the range to older dates, will be added to the master chronology. Match 2 may have as good a fit or even a better one, but will be discounted based on the age determined by ^{14}C dating.

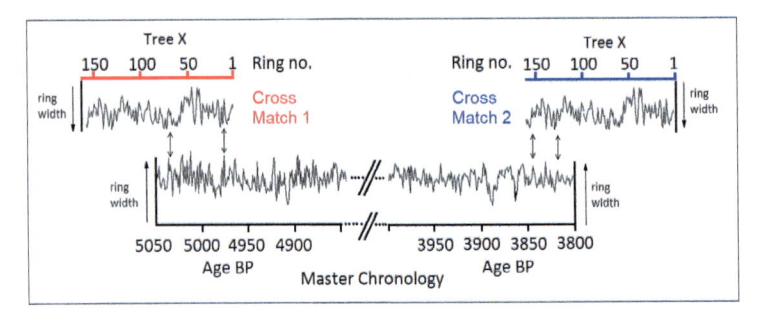

Figure 5.6: *Cross-Matching of a Tree-Ring Pattern with a Master Dendrochronology.*

The intellectual climate, with its absolute commitment to Deep Time, promotes an eagerness to extend the chronologies as far back in time as possible. In his book *A Slice Through Time*, dendrochronologist M. G. L. Baillie acknowledged that:

> Matches between ring patterns, whether between individual trees or between master chronologies, are not perfect 100% matches. The practised dendrochronologist is looking for matches which he/she is willing to accept, based on experience, as correct matches between long ring patterns. [36]

The 'experience' called upon by dendrochronologists is, of course, informed by tree radiocarbon dates and Deep Time preconceptions. In practice, therefore, construction of the tree-ring master chronologies relies on ^{14}C dating, while the ^{14}C method is calibrated by reference to the tree-ring master chronologies. As demonstrated previously, ^{14}C dates are older than real time, and the discrepancy gets larger the nearer the dates move to the giga-catastrophe. The dependence of the tree-ring master chronology on ^{14}C dating for materials older than about 4,000 BP ensures that the ^{14}C dating and dendrochronology remain in sync, but with both recording ages much older than real time. It is rather likely that if ^{14}C dates were calibrated according to the CpT model, a different master tree-ring chronology could be constructed that would also be in good accord with them.

Chapter 5: References and Notes

1. R. H. Brown, 'The interpretation of C-14 dates' in *Origins*, 1979, 6, pp. 30–44.
2. H. W. Scharpenseel and P. Becker-Heidmann, 'Twenty-five years of radiocarbon dating soils: paradigm of erring and learning' in *Radiocarbon*, 1992, 34, pp. 541–9.
3. P. Giem, 'Carbon-14 content of fossil carbon' in *Origins*, 2001, 51, pp. 6–30.
4. R. T. Merrill, M. W. McElhinny and P. L. McFadden, *The Magnetic Field of the Earth: Paleomagnetism, the Core, and the Deep Mantle*, Academic Press, New York, 1996, Ch. 2.
5. R. L. Whitelaw, 'Time, life and history in the light of 15,000 radiocarbon dates' in *Creation Research Society Quarterly*, 1970, 7, pp. 56–71, 83.
6. R. Hefferlin, 'A mathematical formulation of a creationist-flood interpretation of radiocarbon dating' in *Creation Research Society Quarterly*, 1972, 9, pp. 68–71.
7. J. N. Hanson, 'Some mathematical considerations on radiocarbon dating' in *Creation Research Society Quarterly*, 1976, 13, pp. 50–5.
8. (a) K. Kozak, D. Rank, T. Biro, V. Rajner, F. Golder and F. Staudner, 'Retrospective evaluation of tritium fallout by tree-ring analysis' in *Journal of Environmental Radioactivity*, 1993, 19, pp. 67–'77; (b) Y. Yamada, K. Yasuike and K. Komura, 'Temporal variation of tritium concentration in tree-ring cellulose over the past 50 years' in *Journal of Radioanalytical and Nuclear Chemistry*, 2004, 262, pp. 679–83.
9. R. H. Brown, 'C-14 age profiles for ancient sediments and peat bogs' in *Origins*, 1975, 2(1), pp. 6–18.
10. R. H. Brown, 'Correlation of C-14 age with the biblical time scale' in *Origins*, 1990, 17(2), pp. 56–65.
11. R. H. Brown, 'Correlation of C-14 age with real time' in *Creation Research Society Quarterly*, 1992, 29(1), pp. 45–7.
12. R. H. Brown, 'Compatibility of biblical chronology with C-14 age' in *Origins*, 1994, 21(2), pp. 66–79.
13. This date roughly corresponds to that arrived at from genealogical data found in the Septuagint; see: P. J. Ray Jr., 'An evaluation of the numerical variants of the chronogenealogies

of Genesis 5 and 11' in *Origins*, 1985, *12(1)*, pp. 26-37.
14. B. Kemp, 'Egyptian radiocarbon dating: a reply to James Mellaart' in *Antiquity*, 1980, *54*, pp. 25-8.
15. B. Kemp, *Ancient Egypt: Anatomy of a Civilization*, Routledge, London, 1989.
16. S. Bowman, *Radiocarbon Dating*, British Museum, London, 1990.
17. M. G. Hasel, 'Recent developments in Near Eastern chronology and radiocarbon dating' in *Origins*, 2004, *56*, pp. 6-31.
18. D. M. Rohl, *A Test of Time*, Arrow Books, London, 1995, p. 480 et seq.
19. J. Mellaart, 'Egyptian and Near Eastern chronology: a dilemma?' in *Antiquity*, 1979, *53*, pp. 6-22.
20. H. J. Bruins and J. van der Plicht, 'Radiocarbon challenges archaeo-historical time frameworks in the Near East: the Early Bronze Age of Jericho in relation to Egypt' in *Radiocarbon*, 2001, *43*, pp. 1,321-2.
21. E. Braun, 'Proto, Early Dynastic Egypt and Early Bronze I–II of the Southern Levant: some uneasy ^{14}C correlations' in *Radiocarbon*, 2001, *43*, pp. 1,279-95.
22. A. B. Knapp, 'Mesopotamia: History of (Chronology)' in *The Anchor Bible Dictionary*, Volume 4, D. N. Freedman (ed.), Doubleday, 1992, pp. 714-20.
23. H. Haas et al., 'Radiocarbon chronology and the historical calendar in Egypt' in *Chronologies in the Near East: British Archaeological Report S379*, O. Aurenche et al. (eds.), 1987, Part 2, pp. 585-606.
24. A. Mazar, *Archaeology of the Land of the Bible: 10,000-586 BCE*, Doubleday, New York, 1990, p. 28.
25. H. J. Bruins and J. van der Plicht, 'The Minoan Santorini eruption and its ^{14}C position in archaeological strata: preliminary comparison between Ashkelon and Tell el-Dab^{c}a' in *Radiocarbon*, 2017, *59*, pp. 1,295-307.
26. J. Regev, P. de Miroschedji, R. Greenberg, E. Braun, Z. Greenhut and E. Boaretto, 'Proceedings of the 6th International Radiocarbon and Archaeology Symposium' in *Radiocarbon*, E. Boaretto and N. R. Rebolio Franco (eds.), 2012, *54(304)*, pp. 525-66.
27. D. M. Rohl, *From Eden to Exile*, Arrow Books, London, 2002.

28. B. Kemp (ed.), *Amana Reports*, Pt. 1, Egypt Exploration Society, London, 1984, p. 185.
29. O. Aurenche, J. Evin and F. Hours (eds.), *Chronologies du Proche Orient*, Pt. II, Oxford, 1987, p. 606.
30. S. Bourke, E. Lawson, J. Lovell, Q. Hua, U. Zoppi and M. Barbetti, 'The chronology of the Ghassulian Chalcolithic period in the southern Levant: new 14C determinations from Teleilat Ghassul, Jordan' in *Radiocarbon*, 2001, *43(3)*, pp. 1,217–22.
31. J. M. Weinstein, 'Palestinian radiocarbon dating: a reply to James Mellaart' in *Antiquity*, 1980, *54*, pp. 21–4.
32. B. Kemp, 'Egyptian radiocarbon dating: a reply to James Mellaart' in *Antiquity*, 1980, *54*, pp. 25–8.
33. I. E. S. Edwards, C. J. Gadd and N. G. L. Hammond (eds.), *The Cambridge Ancient History, Volume 1, Part 2: Early History of the Middle East*, Cambridge University Press, Cambridge, 1971, p. 994.
34. P. J. Reimer et al., 'IntCal13 and Marine13 radiocarbon age calibration curves 0–50,000 years cal BP' in *Radiocarbon*, 2013, *55(4)*, pp. 1,869–87.
35. For examples of how this works see A. J. Shortland and C. Bronk Ramsey (eds.), *Radiocarbon and the Chronologies of Ancient Egypt*, Oxbow Books, Oxford and Oakville, 2013.
36. M. G. L. Baillie, *A Slice Through Time*, Batsford, London, 1995, p. 21.

Chapter 6

Dinosaur Remnants, Fossils and Compact Time

> *If you thought that science was certain – well, that is just an error on your part.*
> Richard P. Feynman

> *When great changes occur in history, when great principles are involved, as a rule the majority are wrong.*
> Eugene V. Debs

Soft Tissues in Dinosaur Fossils

Compact Time dates reveal that the geologic column was rapidly deposited only thousands of years ago; therefore its fossils and features ought to testify to its being much younger than Deep Time permits. Abundant evidence of many disparate kinds corroborating and supporting this notion does indeed exist. The rapidly deposited sediments, huge igneous formations, flood deposits, mass extinctions etc. were described in Chapter 3. The remarkably prescient remarks of prominent earth scientist Derek Ager that the whole history of the Earth consists of spaced-out, short, sudden happenings, were reported there. A crucial symptom of Compact Time is the residual ^{14}C found in carbon-containing materials throughout the geologic column. The real-time dates of fossils, allowing for the giga-catastrophe, can be estimated from their published ^{14}C content, by means of the CpT relationship – Equation (2) – that's portrayed in Figure 5.2.

Dinosaur fossils are invested with a special glamour! The uncalibrated ^{14}C dates obtained for dinosaur fossils, set out in Tables 2.2–2.4 in Chapter 4, ranged from 21,000–41,000 BP. Some examples were chosen from these and their real-time dates, allowing for the giga-catastrophe, were estimated by means of the CpT model calibration expression. The comparison with conventional Deep Time dates is shown in Table 6.1.

Dinosaur	Conventional Date (Ma BP)	Uncal. ^{14}C Date (BP)	CpT Model Date (BP)
Acrosaurus	65–150	25,750	5,330
Hadrosaur	65–150	31,050	5,340
Triceratops	65–150	39,230	5,350
Triceratops	66	41,010	5,350
Triceratops	66	33,570	5,340

Table 6.1: *CpT Calibrated Dates for Selected Dinosaur Fossils.*

The CpT model gives a properly consistent picture of dinosaur fossils all having ^{14}C dates in a narrow and uniform band from 5,300–5,400 BP. The clear meaning is that all the dinosaurs died and were buried in sediments essentially during the giga-catastrophe.

Dead biological organisms degrade and decompose by the action of microorganisms, by hydrolysis and by oxidation. The rates of these three processes vary depending on the environment of the dead organism; particularly the extent of its exposure to air and water, and the prevailing temperature. All three proceed rapidly in geological time. All rocks are porous to some extent, such that groundwater and oxygen, the key reagents for hydrolytic and oxidative degradation, both of which are small molecules, circulate even in the finest-grained materials, especially in time spans of millions of years. Fossils of all kinds are continually subject to all these degradative processes.

The principal components of the soft tissues of organisms are proteins, lipids, carbohydrates and nucleic acids. Chemically, all these materials have short shelf lives, usually of only a few years. In the laboratory they must be carefully preserved in freezers, in the dark, away from oxygen and protected from contaminants. Chemical stabilisers, antioxidants and other preservative reagents are employed to prevent them decomposing and decaying. In the remains of dead animals, bacteria assimilate the tissues and use them for their own growth and reproduction. Furthermore, hydrolysis converts the biopolymers back to their constituent small-molecule amino acids, carboxylic acids, sugars and bases. Higher temperatures and pressures, and clay catalysts, may cause carbonisation. Additionally, oxidation eventually reduces all these materials to gaseous carbon dioxide accompanied by smaller amounts of the oxides of nitrogen, sulfur and phosphorus. Living organisms continuously make suites of special antioxidant molecules and enzymes to counter these degradative reactions, and also have ongoing repair mechanisms. When the organism dies its antioxidant complement is quickly used up and dissolution proceeds rapidly. From a chemical perspective, survival of soft tissues, proteins, lipids, nucleic acids and biomolecules over millions of years is not credible.

The CpT model ages of dinosaur fossils are of the order of 5,000 BP. This is young enough that some well-protected fossil specimens might not be fully mineralised, and vestiges of soft tissues might remain. On the other hand, the conventional dates for all dinosaur fossils range from sixty-six million years upwards. These ages imply full mineralisation, and that all soft tissues would have degraded, carbonised or converted to their oxidised and hydrolysed components long before the present.

The truly revolutionary science news of the last two decades has been the stream of papers reporting findings of soft tissues in dinosaur fossils. The first reports to attract major attention from the scientific community were those of Dr Mary H. Schweitzer and her team at North Carolina State University.[1,2] Schweitzer discovered soft tissues in a fossil bone from a tyrannosaurus skeleton retrieved from the Hell Creek Formation in Montana. Remarkably, these tissues retained some of their original flexibility, elasticity and resilience. They included unmineralised fragments that, when stretched, returned to their original shape. She observed deeply pigmented structures along with flexible, hollow blood vessels. Her original report was followed up by additional papers showing more such soft dinosaur tissues, and even some protein components. Schweitzer's papers included many convincing high-quality colour photos of the structures (see Figure 6.1).

Knowing the impossibility of soft tissues surviving tens of millions of years, critics countered Schweitzer's reports with a storm of hostile disbelief and scepticism. Her samples were said to be contaminated with modern materials and her methods were claimed to be irreproducible. One dissenting report claimed that what she had observed was a biofilm coating produced by modern bacteria.[3] This contention was shortly debunked.[4] Furthermore, Schweitzer was soon able to confirm the presence of collagen and other proteins that bacteria do not make.[5,2] She recently reported actual peptide sequences for sets of collagen proteins.[6] The extraction of protein, soft tissue, remnant cells and organelle-like structures

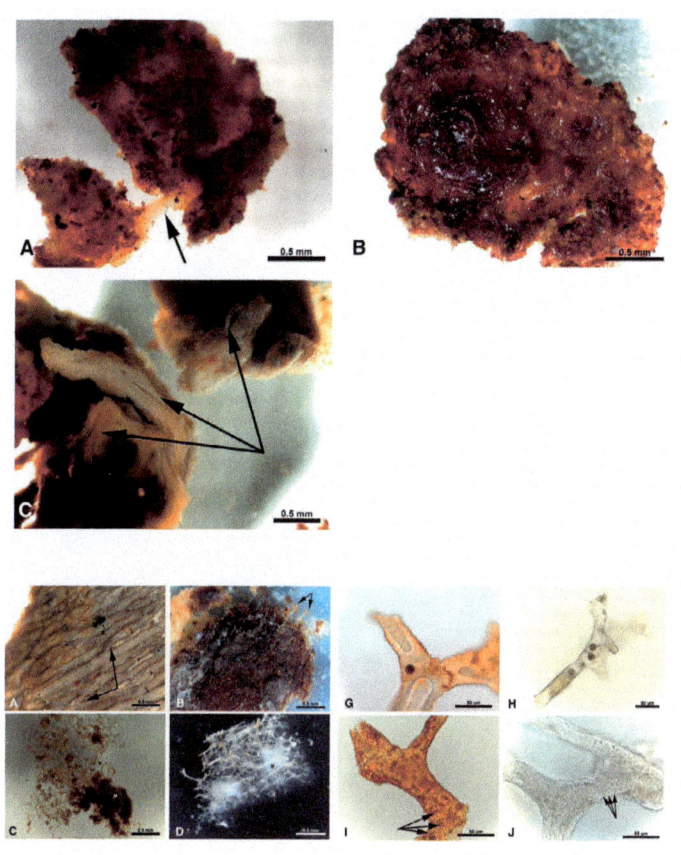

Figure 6.1: *Soft Tissue Fragments from the Marrow Cavity of a T. Rex Femur.*
Photos: M. H. Schweitzer et al., Science, 2005, 307, pp. 1952–5 (reproduced with permission from the American Association for the Advancement of Science).

from dinosaur fossils has been further confirmed.[7,8] Reports began to surface from other research groups of their findings of preserved cellular structures, proteins and even DNA fragments in dinosaur fossils.[9–15] Evidence for the extraction of short segments of ancient DNA from dinosaur fossils has even been reported.[16–18] Schweitzer's findings have been fully vindicated, and a whole field investigating proteins, DNA and soft tissues in ancient fossils has been opened up.[19]

The triceratops horn discovered by Mark Armitage (mentioned in Chapter 2) was not sealed in a solid rock matrix. It was four feet long, buried to about three feet from the surface, and sticking out of fluvial sandstone with water found only another foot lower (see Figure 6.2). Hence, it was exposed to groundwater and oxygen during its entire burial. Pane A of Figure 6.2 shows the horn in situ and Pane B shows intact osteocyte (bone) cells also found in the horn.

Figure 6.2 *Unmineralised Triceratops Brow Horn and Internal Soft Tissues.*
Photos courtesy of Mark Armitage, www.dstri.org [a 501(c)(3) organisation].

These discoveries of soft dinosaur tissues and of protein segments are formidable evidence that the fossils are much younger than their conventional radiometric dates. On the other hand, they accord extremely well with their five-thousand-odd-year CpT dates and robustly support the Compact Time concept. They are impressive evidence implying that these reptiles were all buried during the giga-catastrophe.

Survival of DNA and protein remnants for a few thousand years is not unreasonable in the light of their known chemistry. Proteins have been identified from a number of Egyptian mummies, including some from the First Intermediate period, as old as 4,200 BP.[20,21] The rates of DNA degeneration in papyri and in human remains from Egyptian archaeological sites have been measured.[22] DNA was extracted from modern papyri and from ancient specimens aged up to 3,200 BP. The DNA half-life in papyri was found to be only nineteen to twenty-four years; indicating that none would remain in this medium beyond about a thousand years.

Another scientist studied the decay of DNA in bone specimens of extinct moa birds from New Zealand.[23] The ages of the bones were obtained by radiocarbon dating back to about 8,000 BP, and so will reach older than the true ages. The resulting DNA half-life will therefore be greater than the real half-life, but should give a rough maximum. From the moa bones buried in ground, at the prevailing temperature of about 13°C, the half-life of DNA was estimated to be 521 years. On this basis, no DNA would be detectable beyond about ten half-lives, or five to six thousand years. Several other studies of the rates of DNA and collagen degradation have been published, relying on Deep Time dates. The investigators were innocent of all knowledge of the inadequacy of radiometric dating methods and so they assumed unrealistically old ages for their specimens.

Whether the tiny traces of DNA remaining in Egyptian mummies could really be reliably identified and sequenced has been a matter of vigorous controversy in recent years.[24] A string of articles claiming to detect the minuscule traces of DNA in Egyptian mummies has appeared. This research relies on the extremely sensitive, next-generation sequencing techniques, utilising the amazing polymerase chain reaction (PCR). With this technique, DNA in Graeco-Roman Egyptian mummies (up to 2,800 BP) has been detected.[25] The finding and sequencing of the DNA of Pharaoh Tutankhamun (ca. 3,330 BP) and his relatives gained huge publicity![26] The need to employ the super-powerful amplification of the PCR method demonstrated that natural degradation had reduced the DNA of Egyptian mummies to minuscule levels in only a few thousand years. Survival of DNA to hundreds of thousands or millions of years is certainly ruled out.

From time to time the extraction and sequencing of DNA from specimens reportedly many millions of years old is described. For example, insects entombed in amber reputedly thirty million or more years old have been targeted.[27,28] The PCR cloning method is so extremely potent that contamination from modern DNA is a very serious problem. All such ancient DNA reports need to be approached with great caution.[29,30] However, when the presence of DNA in specimens reputedly this old is confirmed, this is evidence not of some wonderful nature-defying preservation, but that the conventional Deep Time date of the specimen is certainly invalid.

The Deep Timers seem to either ignore the fossil soft tissue evidence, or claim that it's proof that tissues, proteins and DNA actually degrade many orders of magnitude more slowly than the chemistry permits. As mentioned above, rates for tissue degradation are even being deduced based on the conventional stratigraphic timescale. For these faithful adherents, evolutionary Deep Time will always trump physics and chemistry!

Another approach has been to propose special modes of preservation for fossil dinosaur tissues. Schweitzer's proposal that the iron particles found in association with some dinosaur fossils play a role in masking and preserving proteins has been widely quoted.[31] Her laboratory experiments with haemoglobin led to some lengthening of tissue stability. However, her trials with concentrated haemoglobin under laboratory conditions for only two years bore little relation to the field conditions of the fossils. Moreover, any such effect would only apply to fossils associated with iron particles, contrary to the finding of soft tissues in many other circumstances.[32]

Soft Spots in Rock Strata

Specimens of fossil wood, coal, bones and carbonate rocks from essentially every stratum of the geologic column were found to contain ^{14}C levels above background. The over seventy such materials listed by Giem had published ^{14}C/C ratios indicating uncalibrated dates from 44,000–57,000 BP.[33] Technically, the CpT model Equation (2) is only valid to calibrate ^{14}C dates younger than about 40,000 BP. In effect, the calibration curve asymptotically approaches the CpT model age of 5,400 BP. Real-time CpT dates close to 5,400 BP are therefore a reasonable estimate for all these materials. Consequently, the CpT model predicts that evidence of soft tissues, proteins and other comparatively young features should be discernible in samples from every stratum.

More and more such evidence is constantly coming to light! Some pertinent examples are as follows:

- The journal *Geology* reported the discovery of a Miocene age (reputedly 5–23 Ma) fossil baleen whale (Figure 6.3).[34]

A slab of intact baleen from the whale's filter-feeding system was still present. Analysis showed the presence of well-preserved keratin protein fibres, akin to those found in human hair and nails (see Figure 6.3).

- A unique specimen of a blood-engorged mosquito from the Middle Eocene Kishenehn Formation (ca. 40 Ma BP) in Montana, USA was studied. Convincing evidence of the presence of haemoglobin was obtained from analysis of its abdomen. This supported previous reports of the existence of heme-derived porphyrins in terrestrial fossils.[35]
- Edwards and colleagues studied a specimen of a reptile from the Green River Formation, USA (50 Ma BP). Their

Figure 6.3: *Dr Brand with Miocene Baleen Whale Fossil. The reddish area of protein is shown as a microscopic close-up. The electron microscopic view (right) shows the layers of protein fibres.*

maps and spectra revealed that the fossil's skin was entirely comparable to extant reptile skin.[36]
- Lindgren and colleagues examined bone fragments from a Late Cretaceous (100–66 Ma BP) mosasaur (an extinct giant marine lizard) and showed that proteinaceous materials were present.[37] They concluded that primary soft tissues and biomolecules would be found not only in large-sized bones buried in fluvial sandstone environments, but also in relatively small-sized skeletal elements deposited in marine sediments.
- Some of the most remarkable finds were made at a site in Christian Malford, Wiltshire, UK by Dr Philip Wilby and

his team.[38] These excavations in Jurassic Oxford clay (145–201 Ma BP) yielded "thousands of exquisitely preserved ammonites, fish and crustaceans". The team reported collecting two crustaceans, three fish and eight coleoids (squid-like creatures) with soft parts. A cephalopod ink sac and duct with impressions of blood vessels was also obtained (Figure 6.4). "In all cases the soft parts are preserved with exquisite precision, providing tantalizing glimpses of how they functioned." A section through the wall of one coleoid revealed a complex arrangement of muscle fibres. *The Times* of the 19th August 2009 published a remarkable picture of the tiny fossil ink sac alongside a sketch of the squid drawn by an artist with the squid's own fossil ink!

Cephalopod ink sac   Belemnotheutis

Figure 6.4 *Fossil Squid Ink Sac from Wiltshire with an Artist's Drawing of the Squid.*
Photo courtesy of Dr Phil Wilby & Paul Witney [Permit Number CP20/059 British Geological Survey © UKRI 2020. All rights reserved].

The main constituents of squid ink are the pigment melanin[39] and mucus, together with tyrosinase, dopamine and small amounts of free amino acids. The mucus is composed of enzymes, immunoglobulins and glycoproteins. That such delicate and fragile enzymes and tissues could survive five thousand years is very remarkable! Belief in their survival for 145 million years flies in the face of chemical precedents and implies an unshakable faith in Deep Time.

- Russell Vreeland and colleagues at West Chester University in Pennsylvania isolated a bacterium from the Permian (250 Ma BP) Salado Salt Formation at Carlsbad, New Mexico.[40] The bacterium was in a brine inclusion in a salt crystal found 560 metres down a shaft to an underground cavern used for storing nuclear waste. Its 16S ribosomal DNA was still fresh, so they were able to sequence it and show that the organism was part of the lineage of *Bacillus marismortui* and *Virgibacillus pantothenticus*. When Vreeland placed the spores onto growth medium, they returned to life and grew into familiar rod-shaped bacillus bacteria! They have been provisionally named *Bacillus permians* to denote the geological period from which they originated. However, in popular literature they have also been dubbed 'Lazarus bacteria'. John Parkes, a geomicrobiologist at the University of Bristol, is quoted as saying, "All the laws of chemistry tell you that the complex molecules in the spores should have degraded to very simple compounds such as carbon dioxide... Where else are these dormant organisms waiting to be reawakened?"[41]
- George Cody and collaborators studied cuticle materials from a Pennsylvanian (310 Ma BP) scorpion and a Silurian (417 Ma BP) eurypterid (sea scorpion). They found high concentrations of chitin-protein complex in both cases.[42]

Sponges are alleged to be the earliest branching animals, with a fossil record dating back to the Precambrian. Chitin was also discovered in exceptionally well-preserved *Vauxia gracilenta* sponges from the Middle Cambrian Burgess Shale (505 Ma BP).[43]

Figure 6.5: *Diorama of Burgess Shale Sponges and Arthropods.*
Graphic by James St. John; Wikimedia Commons CC-BY-2.0.

The finding of soft tissues, proteins and preserved biological structures in specimens from virtually all strata of the geologic column is in full accord with the residual ^{14}C also found throughout the column. The two sets of findings support and substantiate one another. They reinforce the conclusion that the whole column was deposited rapidly as the result of a giga-catastrophe. They back up the idea that Deep Time is an artificial and invalid construct and should be replaced by Compact Time.

Resolving Anomalies

Conventional radiocarbon dating often gives rise to two or more very different dates for the same specimen. Radio-chronologists often simply dismiss the dates they consider to be 'outliers'. Robert Brown discussed several apparently erratic dates and showed that the anomalies disappear when the Compact Time model is applied.[44] For example, the remains of a musk ox were excavated from frozen mud in the bank of Fairbanks Creek in Alaska. Conventional radiocarbon dating gave the widely divergent ages of 24,140 years for its scalp tissue and 17,210 years for its hair. Hair is replaced much more rapidly than muscle tissue, so the difference could correspond to a minimum age for the animal, but nearly seven thousand years old is absurd! Conversion of these ages to Compact Time with the CpT relationship reduces the difference to about fifty years. The error margin is large of course, but this is certainly a much more reasonable estimate for the age of the ox at death.

Brown collected several similar discordant ^{14}C age determinations that included 26,000 years for hair from the Chekurovka mammoth compared with only 5,610 years for the overlying peat; 11,300 years for ivory from the Pacific mammoth compared with 5000 years for wood fragments in the associated gravel; and 8,900 years for bone collagen from the Ferguson Farm mastodon compared with 6,200 for organic sediment from within its skull cavities.[45] All these anomalies are resolved by applying the Compact Time calibration.

Another curious example concerns data from an excavation in Rampart Cave in the Grand Canyon region.[46] The cave used to be inhabited by ground sloths, and they left their dung pellets there. The hardy excavators counted 39,000 dung pellets that had accumulated on the cave floor. Conventional ^{14}C dating gave 20,000 BP for the top layer, down to 40,000 BP at the bottom. That would mean that during 20,000 years of occupation, the sloths left 1.9 pellets per year in the cave! A small population of sloths persisting for 20,000 years, but only defecating about twice a year. That's an unbelievable scenario! On the other hand, the Compact Time model calibration of these dates gives 5,350–5,270 BP for the sloths dropping their pellets in the cave. That amounts to 1.4 pellets per day for eighty years, which seems a much more reasonable scenario!

1,500 Centuries of Stone Chipping?

Vast and rapid changes have characterised world civilisations during the last five millennia of recorded history. Human imagination knows no bounds, and delights in creativity, inventiveness and innovation. In Europe and the Middle East alone, agriculture has undergone continual modifications, such that even the vegetables, fruits and grains favoured as food have changed, along with their cultivation methods. The ethnic make-up of the races inhabiting virtually every territory has been transformed by mixing and intermarriage as waves of Celtic, Germanic, Viking, Latin, African, Semitic and other peoples have succeeded one another. Burial customs of many different types have been practised. Different materials and styles for clothes, writing and furniture have come and gone. Housing, cities and dwelling places in huge variety have waxed and waned. Modes of transport on land, sea and air have developed through many stages. Manufacturing methods and industries for woods, fibres, metals, stones, slates, tiles, bricks and a host of other materials and commodities have burgeoned and proliferated. Languages have transformed and multiplied, originated and died. Political and religious systems have undergone startling revolutions, reforms and enlightenments. The last fifty centuries have witnessed a rapid procession of novelties, changes, innovations and revolutions in every field of human endeavour.

Conventional radiocarbon dating assigns hugely long-time periods to the Stone Age civilisations that preceded this. Cultural periods pertaining to the Middle and Upper Palaeolithic are listed in Table 6.2 along with their conventional ^{14}C dates.[47] Specimens from the Mousterian epoch were reputedly the oldest, and were radiocarbon dated back to 56,000 BP. Other radiometric methods extended the epoch to about 160,000 BP. This epoch is associated with hunter-gatherer Neanderthals in Europe. Their stone tool assemblages are not much different from those of modern humans. Modern scholars admit that Neanderthals were fully *Homo sapiens*, and that DNA sequencing shows that they intermarried with their anatomically modern neighbours,[48] with whom they lived and were buried. Yet radiometric dating creates the immense time period of 1,200 centuries during which this culture is supposed to have remained one of quiescent hunter-gatherers, with nothing much changing.

The Bohunician, Aurignacian, Gravettian, Solutrean and Magdalenian cultures saw only more hunter-gatherers of anatomically modern Cro-Magnon people groups. The Aurignacians made skilfully sculpted figurines depicting extinct mammals including mammoths, rhinoceros and tarpan, and Venus figurines emphasising reproductive organs. They made pendants, bracelets and ivory beads for bodily ornamentation. The famous paintings in Chauvet Cave in Southern France date from this period. Aurignacian finds also include bone flutes. Emiran stone tools include curved knives similar to those found in the Châtelperronian culture of Western Europe. Their tool industry included worked bone and antlers, plus fine flint blades struck from prepared cores. Also seen throughout the Upper Palaeolithic is a greater degree of tool standardisation, and the use of bone and antler for tools.

Gravettian peoples were also wholly *Homo sapiens*, and tended to live in caves or partly underground dwellings sometimes arranged in small villages. They developed stone tools such as blunt-backed knives, tanged arrowheads, and boomerangs. Gravettian art included numerous cave paintings and small Venus figurines made of clay or ivory.

So, hardly anything happened during the 210 centuries conventional ^{14}C dating allots to the Aurignacian and Gravettian epochs. Just minor developments in stone and bone toolmaking, figurines and art! These populations seem inexplicably quiescent compared to the known frenetic creativity of the modern human race.

The same is true of the hunter-gatherer Solutrean peoples. Further developments in toolmaking took place. Long spear points, with tang and shoulder on one side only, are characteristic implements of this industry. The era's finds include tools, ornamental beads, and bone pins, as well as prehistoric art. The Magdalenian epoch is associated with reindeer hunting and cave art. The main differences from older epochs were novel varieties of stone tools, the development of more bone and ivory implements, tools and weapons, and the cave art.

During these immense time periods, the only innovations of these *Homo sapiens* people groups were flint tool embellishments, bone implement designs, figurines and cave art! Compared to the turbulent changeability of the last 5000 years, practically nothing happened! For the Solutrean and Magdalenian epochs, conventional ^{14}C dating creates another hundred virtually empty centuries!

The Natufian settlement at Jericho provided evidence of somewhat more variety and creativity. It is possible that agriculture was practised and cereals were cultivated. Stone tools were supplemented with heavy stone mortars, and bone industry continued. Evidence of ceremonial burials, archery and beer making was found.

The people groups of these Stone Age epochs were all of

the same *Homo sapiens* species as us, yet radiometric dating places them into nearly 1,500 centuries that are comparatively bare of signs of human inventiveness or progress! The Deep Time scenario paints all these peoples as hunter-gatherers with cultures that remained static and unchanging over immense time periods. This is in glaring contradiction to the creative and progressive disposition of *Homo sapiens* known from the last five-thousand-year era.

Culture/ Archaeology	Regional Variants	^{14}C Date (BP)	CpT Date (BP)
Natufian	Trialetian Mushabian	9,500–12,000	5,070
Hamburgian	Creswellian Federmesser	13,100–15,500	5,200
Magdalenian	Swiderian Khiamian	12,000–17,000	5,170
Solutrean	France Spain Portugal	17,000–22,000	5,260
Gravettian	Epigravettian Périgordian	22,000–33,000	5,300
Aurignacian	Levantine Baradostian	28,000–43,000	5,330
Emiran	Ahmarian Bohunician	42,000–46,000	5,350
Mousterian	Châtelperronian	40,000–56,000	5,350

Table 6.2: *Middle and Upper Palaeolithic Cultures and Periods.*

The fourth column of Table 6.2 records the dates of these Stone Age epochs arrived at by applying the CpT model. With this model, each of the Middle and Upper Palaeolithic epochs occupied no more than one or two centuries. The huge empty stretches of time are contracted down to far more reasonable proportions. The comparatively meagre archaeological remains of Palaeolithic cultures fit easily into a few centuries after the giga-catastrophe.

The Compact Time model depicts scattered people groups in short-term recovery mode from the giga-catastrophe. The empty centuries disappear and the glaring anomaly between the disposition of *Homo sapiens* during the Stone Age and after it is removed.

Know-how from laboratory work with tissues, proteins and DNA is emphatic that these fragile materials can't survive natural degradative processes for millions of years. The findings of well-preserved and bona fide soft tissues and biopolymers in dinosaur fossils are therefore ground breaking. They are formidable evidence that these fossils can't be millions of years old. The numerous reports of soft tissues and proteins surviving in fossil specimens from many of the strata in the geologic column expose the invalidity of their Deep Time dates. Contrariwise, these discoveries offer impressive support for the Compact Time chronology. Furthermore, adoption of CpT ages helps to resolve erratic results thrown up by conventional radiocarbon dating. Compaction of the timescale rids the Early Bronze Age of troublesome empty centuries. Furthermore, Stone Age *Homo sapiens* populations no longer rattle around in achingly deserted 1,500-century stretches of time!

Chapter 6: References and Notes

1. (a) M. H. Schweitzer, J. L. Wittmeyer, J. R. Horner and J. K. Toporski, 'Soft-tissue vessels and cellular preservation in *Tyrannosaurus rex*' in *Science*, 2005, *307*, pp. 1,952–5; (b) M. H. Schweitzer, J. L. Wittmeyer and J. R. Horner, 'Soft tissue and cellular preservation in vertebrate skeletal elements from the Cretaceous to the present' in *Proceedings: Biological Sciences*, 2007, *274 (1607)*, pp. 183–97.
2. M. H. Schweitzer, W. Zheng, C. L. Organ, R. Avci, Z. Suo, L. M. Freimark, V. S. Lebleu, M. B. Duncan, M. G. Vander Heiden, J. M. Neveu, W. S. Lane, J. S. Cottrell, J. R. Horner, L. C. Cantley, R. Kalluri and J. M. Asara, 'Biomolecular characterization and protein sequences of the Campanian hadrosaur *B. canadensis*' in *Science*, 2009, *324*, pp. 626–31.
3. T. G. Kaye, G. Gaugler and Z. Sawlowicz, 'Dinosaurian soft tissues interpreted as bacterial biofilms' in *PLOS ONE*, 2008, *3(7)*, e2808.
4. J. E. Peterson, M. E. Lenczewski and R. P. Scherer, 'Influence of microbial biofilms on the preservation of primary soft tissue in fossil and extant archosaurs' in *PLOS ONE*, 2010, *5(10)*, e1334 [doi.org/10.1371/journal.pone.0013334].
5. M. H. Schweitzer, A. E. Moyer and W. Zheng, 'Testing the hypothesis of biofilm as a source for soft tissue and cell-like structures preserved in dinosaur bone' in *PLOS ONE*, 2016, *11(2)*, e0150238/1–e0150238/18.
6. E. R. Schroeter, C. J. DeHart, T. P. Cleland, W. Zheng, P. M. Thomas, N. L. Kelleher, M. Bern and M. H. Schweitzer, 'Expansion for the *Brachylophosaurus canadensis* Collagen I sequence and additional evidence of the preservation of Cretaceous protein' in *Journal of Proteome Research*, 2017, *16(2)*, pp. 920–32.
7. J. D. San Antonio, M. H. Schweitzer, S. T. Jensen, R. Kalluri, M. Buckley and J. P. R. O. Orgel, 'Dinosaur peptides suggest mechanisms of protein survival' in *PLOS ONE*, 2011, *6(6)*, e20381.
8. T. P. Cleland, E. R. Schroeter et al., 'Mass spectrometry and antibody-based characterization of blood vessels from *Brachylophosaurus canadensis*' in *Journal of Proteome Research*, 2015, *14(12)*, pp. 5,252–62.

9. R. Pawlicki, A. Dkorbel and H. Kubiak, 'Cells, collagen fibrils and vessels in dinosaur bone' in *Nature*, 1966, *211*, pp. 655–7.
10. R. Pawlicki, 'Histochemical demonstration of DNA in osteocytes from dinosaur bones' in *Folia Histochemica et Cytobiologica*, 1995, *33*, pp. 183–6.
11. R. Pawlicki and M. Nowogrodzka-Zagórska, 'Blood vessels and red blood cells preserved in dinosaur bones' in *Annals of Anatomy*, 1998, *180*, pp. 73–7 (doi:10.1016/S0940-9602(98)80140-4).
12. T. Lingham-Soliar, 'A unique cross section through the skin of the dinosaur *Psittacosaurus* from China showing a complex fibre architecture' in *Proceedings: Biological Sciences*, 2008, *275*, pp. 775–80.
13. T. Lingham-Soliar and G. Plodowski, 'The integument of *Psittacosaurus* from Liaoning Province, China: taphonomy, epidermal patterns and color of a ceratopsian dinosaur' in *Naturwissenschaften*, 2010, *97*, pp. 479–86.
14. M. H. Armitage and K. L. Anderson, 'Soft sheets of fibrillar bone from a fossil of the supraorbital horn of the dinosaur *Triceratops horridus*' in *Acta Histochimica*, 2013, *115*, pp. 603–8.
15. A. M. Bailleul, W. Zheng, J. R. Horner, B. K. Hall, C. M. Holliday and M. H. Schweitzer, 'Evidence of proteins, chromosomes and chemical markers of DNA in exceptionally preserved dinosaur cartilage' in *National Science Review*, 2020, *7*, pp. 815-822, [https://doi.org/10.1093/nsr/nwz206.]
16. M. H. Schweitzer, W. Zheng, T. P. Cleland and M. Bern, 'Molecular analyses of dinosaur osteocytes support the presence of endogenous molecules' in *Bone*, 2013, *52(1)*, pp. 414–23.
17. S. R. Woodward, N. J. Weyand and M. Bunnell, 'DNA sequence from Cretaceous period bone fragments' in *Science*, 1994, *266(5188)*, pp. 1,229–32.
18. A. M. Bailleul, W. Zheng, J. R. Horner, B. K. Hall, C. M. Holliday and M. H. Schweitzer, 'Evidence of proteins, chromosomes and chemical markers of DNA in exceptionally preserved dinosaur cartilage' in *National Science Review*, 12th January 2020, https://doi.org/10.1093/nsr/nwz206
19. For a review see M. H. Schweitzer, 'Soft tissue preservation in terrestrial Mesozoic vertebrates' in *Annual Review of Earth and Planetary Sciences*, 2011, *39*, pp. 187–216.

20. J. Jones, M. Mirzaei, P. Ravishankar, D. Xavier, D. S. Lim, D. H. Shin, R. Bianucci and P. A. Haynes, 'Identification of proteins from 4,200-year-old skin and muscle tissue biopsies from ancient Egyptian mummies of the First Intermediate period shows evidence of acute inflammation and severe immune response' in *Philosophical Transactions of the Royal Society*, Series A, 2016, *374*, 20150373/1-20150373/19.
21. R. A. Barraco, 'Preservation of proteins in mummified tissues' in *American Journal of Physical Anthropology*, 1978, *48(4)*, pp. 487–91.
22. I. Marota, C. Basile, M. Ubaldi and F. Rollo, 'DNA decay rate in papyri and human remains from Egyptian archaeological sites' in *American Journal of Physical Anthropology*, 2002, *117(4)*, pp. 310–18.
23. M. E. Allentoft, M. Collins, D. Harker, J. Haile, C. L. Oskam, M. L. Hale, P. F. Campos, J. A. Samaniego, M. T. P. Gilbert, E. Willerslev, G. Zhang, P. R. Scofield, R. N. Holdaway and M. Bunce, 'The half-life of DNA in bone: measuring decay kinetics in 158 dated fossils' in *Proceedings of the Royal Society B*, 2012, *279*, pp. 4,724–33.
24. J. Marchant, 'Ancient DNA: curse of the pharaoh's DNA' in *Nature*, 2011, *472*, pp. 404–6.
25. R. Khairat, M. Ball, C-C. H. Chang, R. Bianucci, A. G. Nerlich, M. Trautmann, S. Ismail, G. M. L. Shanab, A. M. Karim, Y. Z. Gad et al., 'First insights into the metagenome of Egyptian mummies using next-generation sequencing' in *Journal of Applied Genetics*, 2013, *54(3)*, pp. 309–25.
26. Z. Hawass, Y. Z. Gad, S. Ismail, R. Khairat, D. Fathalla, N. Hasan, A. Ahmed, H. Elleithy, M. Ball, F. Gaballah, S. Wasef, M. Fateen, H. Amer, P. Gostner, A. Selim, A. Zink and C. M. Pusch, 'Ancestry and pathology in King Tutankhamun's family' in *Journal of the American Medical Association*, 2010, *303*, pp. 638–47.
27. P. Veiga-Crespo, M. Poza, M. Prieto-Alcedo and T. G. Villa, 'Ancient genes of *Saccharomyces cerevisiae*' in *Microbiology*, 2004, *150(7)*, pp. 2,221–7.
28. J. J. Austin, A. B. Smith, R. A. Fortey and R. H. Thomas, 'Ancient DNA from amber inclusions: a review of the evidence' in *Ancient Biomolecules*, 1998, *2(2–3)*, pp. 167–76.
29. T. Lindahl, 'Instability and decay of the primary structure of

DNA' in *Nature*, 1993, *362*, pp. 709–15.
30. M. Hoss, 'Ancient DNA: Neanderthal population genetics' in *Nature*, 2000, *404*, pp. 453–4.
31. M. H. Schweitzer, W. Zheng, T. P. Cleland, M. B. Goodwin, E. Boatman, E. Theil, M. A. Marcus and S. C. Fakra, 'A role for iron and oxygen chemistry in preserving soft tissues, cells and molecules from Deep Time' in *Proceedings of the Royal Society B*, 2014, *281(1775)*, 20132741, doi:10.1098/rspb.2013.2741
32. Schweitzer attributes the preservation to activity of free radicals released by Fenton chemistry of iron particles. However, free radicals couple very rapidly with oxygen and are then the prime agents in oxidative degradation of lipids and other biological materials. See for example J. A. Howard in *Free Radicals*, J. K. Kochi (ed.), Wiley, New York, Volume 2, 1973, Ch. 12, pp. 4–57. It is far more likely, therefore, that in the long term, free-radical reactive oxygen species (ROS) would accelerate degradation of soft tissues.
33. P. Giem, 'Carbon-14 content of fossil carbon' in *Origins*, 2001, *51*, pp. 6–30.
34. L. Brand et al., 'Whales bite the (diatom) dust' in *Geology*, 2004, *32(2)*, p. 165.
35. D. E. Greenwalt, Y. S. Goreva, S. M. Siljeström, T. Rose and R. E. Harbach, 'Hemoglobin-derived porphyrins preserved in a Middle Eocene blood-engorged mosquito' in *Proceedings of the National Academy of Sciences of the United States of America*, 2013, *110(46)*, pp. 18,496–500.
36. N. P. Edwards, H. E. Barden, B. E. van Dongen, P. L. Manning, P. L. Larson, U. Bergmann, W. I. Sellers and R. A. Wogelius, 'Infrared mapping resolves soft tissue preservation in 50 million year-old reptile skin' in *Proceedings of the Royal Society B*, 2011, *278(1,722)*, pp. 3,209–18.
37. J. Lindgren et al., 'Microspectroscopic evidence of Cretaceous bone proteins' in *PLOS ONE*, 2011, *6*, e19445.
38. P. R. Wilby, K. Duff, K. Page and S. Martin, 'Preserving the unpreservable: a lost world rediscovered at Christian Malford, UK' in *Geology Today*, 2008, *24(3)*, pp. 95–8.
39. K. Glass, S. Ito, P. R. Wilby, T. Sota, A. Nakamura, C. R. Bowers, J. Vinther, S. Dutta, R. Summons, D. E. G. Briggs, K. Wakamatsu and J. D. Simon, 'Direct chemical evidence for

eumelanin pigment from the Jurassic period' in *PNAS*, 2012, *109*(26), pp. 10,218–23.
40. R. H. Vreeland, W. D. Rosenzweig and D. W. Powers, 'Isolation of a 250 million-year-old halotolerant bacterium from a primary salt crystal' in *Nature*, 2000, *407*, pp. 897–900.
41. Quoted by A. Coghlan, 'Eternal life' in *New Scientist*, 18th October 2000.
42. G. D. Cody, N. S. Gupta, D. E. G. Briggs, A. L. D. Kilcoyne, R. E. Summons, F. Kenig, R. E. Plotnick and A. C. Scott, 'Molecular signature of chitin-protein complex in Paleozoic arthropods' in *Geology*, 2011, *39(3)*, pp. 255–8.
43. H. Ehrlich, V. V. Bazhenov, J. K. Rigby, J. P. Botting, M. V. Tsurkan, C. Werner, P. Schwille, Z. Petrášek, A. Pisera, P. Simon et al., 'Discovery of 505-million-year-old chitin in the basal demosponge *Vauxia gracilenta*' in *Scientific Reports*, 2013, *3*, p. 3,497.
44. R. H. Brown, 'Correlation of C-14 age with the biblical time scale' in *Origins*, 1990, *17(2)*, pp. 56–65.
45. R. H. Brown, 'C-14 Age profiles for ancient sediments and peat bogs' in *Origins*, 1975, *1(2)*, pp. 6–18.
46. A. Long and P. S. Martin, 'Death of American ground sloths' in *Science*, 1974, *186*, pp. 638–40.
47. Radiocarbon dates are given in G. Clark, *World Prehistory*, Cambridge University Press, Cambridge, 1969, and are in essential agreement with more modern ones on Wikipedia.
48. S. Pääbo, *Neanderthal Man: In Search of Lost Genomes*, Basic Books, New York, 2014.

Chapter 7

Outcomes and Implications

In this age of specialization men who thoroughly know one field are often incompetent to discuss another. The great problems of the relations between one and another aspect of human activity have for this reason been discussed less and less in public. When we look at the past great debates on these subjects we feel jealous of those times, for we should have liked the excitement of such argument. The old problems, such as the relation of science and religion, are still with us, and I believe present as difficult dilemmas as ever, but they are not often publicly discussed because of the limitations of specialization.

Richard P. Feynman

Compact Time and the Geologic Column

The Compact Time chronology implies that the Pleistocene epoch (Ice Age), possibly also including some of the Pliocene and the Palaeolithic eras, occupy only hundreds of years of time after the giga-catastrophe. The rest of the geologic column, including the remainder of the Cenozoic, Mesozoic and Palaeozoic eras, is compacted into the short duration of the giga-catastrophe and its aftermath as depicted in Figure 7.1. The geologic column portrays the rapid successive burials of populations of taxa that, before the giga-catastrophe, *all existed together*, in their appropriate ecological niches. The notion that the different strata accumulated extremely slowly over long ages is seen to be untenable and needs to be given up. The much-cherished belief that the strata from the Cambrian to the present preserve a record of the slow evolutionary transformations of biological organisms is seen as mistaken.

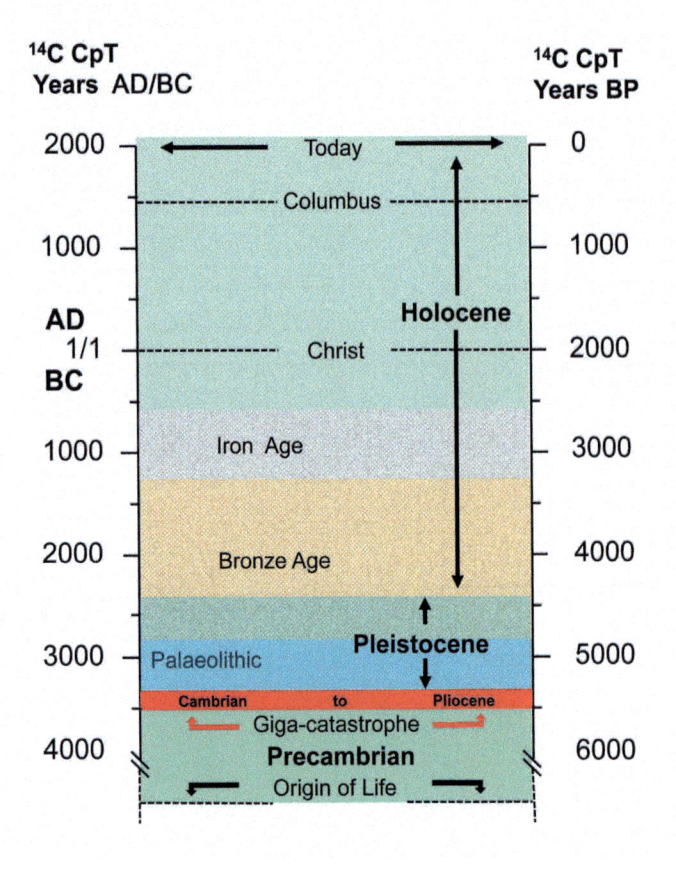

Figure 7.1: *Radiocarbon-Derived Compact Time Chronology for Earth History.*

This Compact Time interpretation of the geological record is not as revolutionary as at first appears. Charles Darwin readily admitted that the fossil record, particularly the lack of the "innumerable intermediate forms" he expected, presented problems. He put this down to the incompleteness of the record in his day. Now, after 150 more years of intense palaeontological investigations, the same characteristics persist. These are the sudden appearance of species, their remaining practically unchanged throughout their time in the column (referred to as biological stasis), and their sudden disappearance. University of Chicago palaeontologist David M. Raup summed up the fossil depositional features this way:

> *Most people assume that fossils provide important [evidence] in favour of the Darwinian interpretation of the history of life. Unfortunately, this is not strictly true. Rather than gradual unfolding of life… species appear in the sequence very suddenly, show little or no change during their existence in the record, then abruptly [disappear].*[1]

Biologist and palaeontologist Niles Eldredge made similar observations:

> *No wonder paleontologists shied away from evolution for so long. It never seemed to happen. Assiduous collecting up cliff faces yields zigzags, minor oscillations, and the very occasional slight accumulation of change – over millions of years, at a rate too slow to really account for the prodigious change that has occurred in evolutionary history. When we do see the introduction of evolutionary novelty, it usually shows up with a bang, and often with no firm evidence that the organisms did not evolve elsewhere.*[2]

These characteristic features prompted him, along with Stephen Gould, to propose the punctuated equilibrium scenario. Even ardent evolution advocate Ernst Mayr, one of the 20th century's leading evolutionary biologists, wrote:

> *Given the fact of evolution, one would expect the fossils to document steady change from ancestral forms to the descendants. But this is not what the palaeontologist finds… New types often appear quite suddenly, and their immediate ancestors are absent in the earlier geological strata. The discovery of unbroken series of species changing gradually into descending species is very rare.*[3]

Given the Compact Time chronology and burial scenario, the sudden appearance of species, their biological stasis, the lack of transitional species and the sudden disappearances are features of the geological column that make good sense. The sudden appearance of organisms from all the major taxa including kingdoms, phyla, classes and orders in the Cambrian Explosion, the Mammalian Radiation in the Palaeocene, the Angiosperm Big Bloom in the Cretaceous, and other similar radiations, were not 'appearances'. Rather, they were the sudden burials of large ecological units of flora and fauna. The 'big five' and other mass extinctions are easily understood as mass burials during the giga-catastrophe. The habitats of creatures such as trilobites and dinosaurs were destroyed during the giga-catastrophe, so they were not able to re-establish themselves afterwards.

The lack of change in organisms is represented, for example, by fossil sea urchins that show no change from the Cretaceous to the present, by fossil ferns that are unchanged from the Carboniferous to the present, by horseshoe crab fossils from the Cambrian that are virtually identical to modern ones, or by nautilus fossils from the Early Cambrian that closely match the modern nautilus. Take away the hundreds of millions of years and this biological stasis makes good sense. Compact Time also solves the puzzle of 'living fossils' that 'disappeared' from the fossil record for huge stretches of time. For example, coelacanths were thought to have gone extinct sixty-six million years ago, until a living specimen belonging to the order was discovered in 1938. Another example, the Wollemi pine (related to the monkey puzzle tree), was known from fossils in the Jurassic period. Then a grove of Wollemi pines was discovered in 1994 in the Blue Mountains of Australia. The incongruity of such finds evaporates when Deep Time gives way to Compact Time.

Countless fossil trees with their trunks passing through many strata appear in the geologic column. These 'polystrate' trees are often found in coal measures. Examples are documented from the Joggins Formation in Nova Scotia (see Figure 7.2) and from many other locations in Europe, the USA and Australia.

Figure 7.2: *Polystrate Fossil Trees.*
Photos: (A) Michael C. Rygel; Wikimedia Commons CC-BY-3.0; (B) Bay of Fundy, courtesy of Dr Ariel Roth; (C) Joggins Formation, courtesy of Dr Harold Coffin, with permission of the Geoscience Research Institute.

Had these trees been buried in successive strata over hundreds of thousands of years, the trunk exposed after deposition of the first layer of sediment would have decayed away long before the next layer of sediment had accumulated. On the other hand, their preservation is just as expected from their burial by successive rapid depositional events during the giga-catastrophe.

The comparative paucity of intermediate species demonstrating transitions from ancestral forms to descendants is well known. The search for fossils of 'missing links' continues unabated and new discoveries attract huge publicity. It's true that popular books, websites and museums display many iconic exhibits purporting to show transitional forms. However, the evidence is almost always of minor variations of size or pigmentation. Fossils of alternate varieties of species, genera and even some families can certainly be found. Such microevolutionary changes can be accomplished in only a few generations, and are compatible with Compact Time. It is the absence of fossil forms demonstrating the evolution of the higher taxonomic ranks – order, class, phylum and kingdom – that poses the problem for Deep Time.

Where are the Fossils of Modern Human Beings?

During the giga-catastrophe, whole populations of creatures were engulfed with great rapidity. Shouldn't palaeontologists find, therefore, human fossils widely distributed in the strata? Several factors are unfavourable for this. The anatomy and physiology of primates means they have poor potential for fossilisation. Primates don't have hard shells or large, solid bones, so their bodies tend to float and bloat in water. They become prey for scavengers and microorganisms as well as hydrolytic and oxidative degradative processes. Special circumstances of rapid burial and protection are needed for any chance of mineralisation. The vast majority of all fossils are found in sediments laid down from water; consequently, primate fossils are rare and amount to only a minuscule proportion of the fossil record. Most such fossils consist of fragments of jaws or teeth. Statistically valid interpretations of the significance of this scanty material are problematic. The size of the human population before the giga-catastrophe is completely unknown. It would depend on the length of the time period from the giga-catastrophe back to the origin of human life. This is addressed in a subsequent section.

When considering human fossils, the default mode for conventional dating of fossils needs to be recollected. If a specimen is discovered outside the epoch or sub-epoch in the geologic column established for it by evolutionary geoscience, then it is regularly discounted or 'reinterpreted'. The 'out of Africa' scenario currently dominates accounts of human evolution, and this places anatomically modern *Homo sapiens* in strata no older than about 300,000 BP on the conventional timescale. 'Reinterpretation' is the fate that has overtaken most discoveries of modern *Homo sapiens* in strata older than this. In practice, this means the fossil will be considered as intrusive; that is, buried there, either by human agency or by natural forces. Not surprisingly, most reported discoveries of ancient *Homo sapiens* fossils date from the 19th or early 20th centuries, before the current ossification of evolutionary scenarios and the deployment of coercive methods to preserve them.

It is not often that the reinterpretation process leaves a paper trail. However, the saga of Dr Hans Reck's discovery in 1913 of a complete modern skeleton in the Upper Bed II of Olduvai Gorge is exceptional. The reinterpretation process is illustrated by the series of papers the palaeontologists sent to the journal *Nature*.[4] Reck was an experienced professional and carefully sought evidence of burial or earth movements. He reported that the bed showed no sign of disturbance, that there was no evidence of a grave, that the skeleton was parallel to the layers of stone containing it; just as were all the other remains of extinct animals contained in the same stratum. Reck returned to Germany, taking the skeleton with him to Munich. Louis Leakey was interested in the fossil and visited Reck in Germany several times to inspect it. In 1931, after the First World War, Reck, Leakey and a group of palaeontologists revisited the site in Olduvai where the skeleton had been discovered. The others agreed with Reck's original conclusion that the skeleton was not intrusive and sent a letter to *Nature* confirming this.

Bed II of Olduvai Gorge is conventionally dated at about 1.2 Ma BP, so this discovery drew a lot of flak from the human anthropology community. In 1932, Professor P. G. H. Boswell of Imperial College, London obtained from Munich some of the material in which the skeleton had been packed. From his examination of this, and tests of the organic content of the fossils, he decided the skeleton was intrusive. In the next two years, Leakey and others visited Munich for more tests. Then, on the basis of tests carried out on laboratory material twenty years after the discovery of the skeleton, Reck, Leakey and three other scientists published an article revoking previous evidence from the actual Olduvai site and concluding that the skeleton was intrusive. The fossil was then conveniently forgotten, so that when in 1974 Reiner Protsch attempted to radiocarbon date the skeleton, only a few bone fragments thought to belong to it could be found. Protsch claimed that insufficient bone was available to fill his counter, and no precautions against contamination were mentioned, but a radiocarbon date of 16,920 years was published.[5] The reinterpretation process was thus brought to a conclusion entirely satisfactory from the standpoint of human evolutionary theory. Many years later, in 2004, Protsch's radiocarbon dating of human fossils was revealed as another of the frauds periodically plaguing palaeoanthropology.[6]

There are, however, many reports about fragmentary fossils of modern *Homo sapiens*, plus stone and bone tools and other artefacts, being uncovered in pre-Pleistocene strata. Cremo and Thompson made a long, comprehensive list of more than ninety such finds, together with lengthy evaluations of their authenticity or otherwise.[4b] In point of fact, these finds amount to impressive evidence of widespread human habitation and activity across many strata. Most of these finds are dismissed by mainstream palaeontology. Grounds for dismissal might be that no professional palaeontologist was present at the site of discovery so tell-tale signs of burial would have been missed, or that radiocarbon dating had shown them to be young.

Fossils with admittedly modern appearance found in ancient strata are simply classified as belonging to extinct apes. For example, in 1965 an upper arm bone (humeral fragment) was discovered at Kanapoi in Kenya in sediments dated at 4–4.5 Ma BP. Measurements by several groups of anatomists agreed it was essentially indistinguishable from modern humeri. A trail of fossil footprints was uncovered by Mary Leakey at Laetoli in northern Tanzania in 1979.[7] The prints showed the raised arch, rounded heel and forward-pointing big toe characteristic of modern *Homo sapiens*. Experts pronounced them indistinguishable from those of modern humans walking in damp sand. However, the layers of volcanic ash in which they were found were dated by the potassium-argon method to 3.6–3.8 Ma BP, so the footprints were said to have been made by ape-like australopithecines.

Rupe and Sanford have published a comprehensive survey and evaluation of ancient human and hominin fossils.[8] They describe more finds of very ancient *Homo sapiens* fossils and footprints, and critique the unsound dating practices. An extremely interesting project would be to carry out radiocarbon dating on the finds of fossil hominins such as the various australopithecines, *Homo habilis* and related materials.

When asked what would destroy his confidence in the theory of evolution, J. B. S. Haldane, who introduced the 'primordial soup' concept, is reputed to have said, "Fossil rabbits in the Precambrian." This answer became popular imagery in debates about evolutionary biology in the '90s and 2000s. Haldane's answer reveals an almost endearingly naive innocence about how palaeontology works. However genuine, any such fossils would be dismissed out of hand as intrusive. At the present time, any palaeontologist who discovered out-of-place rabbits, or *Homo sapiens* fossils, and officially attributed dates to them significantly older than evolutionary theory demands, would risk his or her reputation. He or she would be written off as incompetent for not sighting evidence that they were intrusive, his or her funding would dry up or, worse still, he or she would be branded a fraud.

Precambrian Strata and the Age of the Earth

Deep Time is an absolute necessity for the neo-Darwinian evolutionary synthesis. The geologic column, from the Cambrian to the present, does not provide evidence of this. What, then, about the Precambrian strata that represent time before the giga-catastrophe? There are only a few radiocarbon measurements for specimens of Precambrian age. Giem's list includes some Precambrian graphite samples from Finland, for which $^{14}C/C$ ratios of about 0.05 pMC had been measured.[9] For diamonds, $^{14}C/C$ ratios of about 0.09 pMC have been reported (see Chapter 2). These levels of radiocarbon are scarcely above the AMS instrument background. Neither the conventional IntCal13 calibrated ^{14}C dating method, nor the Compact Time relationship, is valid for converting these Precambrian $^{14}C/C$ ratios to real-time ages. That's because the level of radiocarbon in the Precambrian atmosphere is not known accurately. However, the half-life of ^{14}C

is 'only' 5,730 years, so the finding of *any* residual radiocarbon in Precambrian specimens implies a short duration of only thousands of years for the era. A systematic study of radiocarbon in carbonaceous remains of Precambrian age would be a worthwhile research project. Information about the quantity and stratigraphic and geographic distribution of Precambrian radiocarbon might enable the atmospheric and marine levels to be estimated, and hence a timescale to be constructed.

Precambrian strata contain sedimentary and igneous rocks resembling modern counterparts together with some unique types. All minerals except oxides are unstable in chemical weathering. The ions derived from weathering when transported into areas of sedimentation recombine, mostly forming clay minerals. Clays are as abundant in the Early Precambrian as at present. Precambrian strata contain very few fossils. There are collections of very diverse and exotic soft-bodied forms in a variety of locations worldwide that are conventionally dated to between 635 and 542 Ma BP. These Ediacaran or Vendian species are not thought to be ancestral to the biota of the Cambrian, and were probably also buried by the giga-catastrophe.

Apart from this, almost all the sparse reports of Precambrian fossils deal with 'microfossils' of microscopic organisms. Stromatolites are mound-like objects with a characteristic laminated structure. They are thought to form by precipitation of mineral matter on the enlarging surfaces of microbial communities. Stromatolites are known from the Bulawayan group of Early Precambrian age and are widespread in the Middle and Late Precambrian. These fossil stromatolites bear a marked resemblance to modern ones forming at Hamelin Pool near Shark Bay, Australia. Microfossils derived from bacteria and microbial organisms transported into rocks by groundwater have been identified in many Precambrian sediments. The Onverwacht and Fig Tree groups of the Swaziland system of South Africa are considered to be the oldest relatively unmetamorphosed rocks known. Numerous globular, filamentous and rod-like microfossils have been found in cherts and shales from both these rock groups. Undoubted microfossils of diverse and structurally complex microorganisms are relatively abundant in rocks of Middle Precambrian age.

A variety of 'chemical fossils', also known as 'biological markers', have been identified in the extractable fractions from Precambrian cherts and shales. These were isoprenoids such as pristane and phytane, steranes, fatty acids and metal chelated porphyrins. They point towards a biological origin for much of this material from the Early, Middle and Late Precambrian formations. Non-extractable, partly graphitic materials known as kerogen and thucholite occur in many formations. Fractionation of the stable carbon isotopes ^{12}C and ^{13}C occurs in living systems and is measured in terms of δ^{13}C. Negative values indicate material of biological origin, and near-zero or positive values are characteristic of inorganic carbon-containing remains. Several Precambrian formations contain kerogen with the negative δ^{13}C values characteristic of biogenic material. Even the supposedly 3.8 Ga rocks of the Isua Greenstone Belt of Western Greenland show this.

This is practically all the evidence pertaining to living organisms that has been discovered from Precambrian strata supposedly covering nearly four billion years. Ancestral links to the abundant biota that suddenly appeared in the Cambrian Explosion have never been discovered. Fossils have not been located of either more primitive creatures or of intermediate organisms. Precambrian terrains are complex, and cycles involving apparent processes have been observed. Vast ocean-sized basins of 'primordial soup', as the hotbed for abiogenesis, have been proposed and might be expected to give rise to fossilised or graphitised reservoirs or beds of primordial molecules and proto-cells. No vast remnants have been found in shales, clays, evaporites or any Precambrian sedimentary environments. Neither have mineralised remains from 'RNA world'-type self-assembling, self-replicating biopolymer colonies been encountered in Precambrian rocks. Clays, particularly montmorillonite, have been proposed as catalytic templates for the condensation polymerisation of biological molecules, leading to self-replicating 'proto-cells'. Clays are abundant in Precambrian strata, but none have been discovered containing the large-extent deposits of graphitised, carbonised or other polymerised remains that could be attributed to such activity.

It seems inescapable that a multitude of complex living organisms appeared very suddenly in the time before the giga-catastrophe. Definite data about the duration of the Precambrian era is lacking. More radiocarbon data is needed to determine if all or any of it extended for only thousands of years. The giga-catastrophe buried representatives of all the taxonomic categories. Putative macroevolutionary processes would not have had the Deep Time needed for development of that huge diversity of species. Certainly, no record of this has been left in Precambrian strata. So, where did the living species come from? The notion that they were 'beamed in' by some amazing teleportation process, or some 'panspermia' shower from elsewhere in the universe, can be dismissed. Earth itself is manifestly the best-equipped and best-prepared place to support living things or any supposed molecular precursors to life.

Chapter 7: References and Notes

1. D. M. Raup, 'Conflicts between Darwin and paleontology' in *Field Museum of Natural History Bulletin*, 1979, Volume 50, pp. 22-9.
2. N. Eldredge, *Reinventing Darwin*, Orion Publishing, London, 1996, p. 95.
3. E. W. Mayr, *What Evolution Is*, Basic Books, New York, 2001, p. 16.
4. For details and references see (a) M. Bowden, *Ape-Men*, second edition, Sovereign Publications, Bromley, 1977, pp. 187-93; (b) M. A. Cremo and R. L. Thompson, *Forbidden Archeology*, Bhaktivedanta Book Trust, Los Angeles, 2005, pp. 628-49.
5. R. Protsch, 'The age and stratigraphic position of Olduvai Hominid I' in *Journal of Human Evolution*, 1974, 3, pp. 379-85.
6. Note that accusations of fraudulent dating were levelled at Professor Reiner Protsch von Zieten, who was suspended in 2004 and forced to retire early from his position as director of the Institute of Anthropology and Human Genetics for Biology at Goethe University in Frankfurt.
7. M. D. Leakey, 'Footprints in the ashes of time' in *National Geographic*, 1979, *155*, pp. 446-57.
8. C. Rupe and J. C. Sanford, *Contested Bones*, FMS Publications, 2017.
9. P. Giem, 'Carbon-14 content of fossil carbon' in *Origins*, 2001, *51*, pp. 6-30.

Chapter 8

Compact Time and Ideology

To what or to whom do we owe our existence? This has to be the starting point for people who take life seriously – whether scientists or not. We cannot rest without the answer because absolutely everything of importance is riding on it.
Douglas Axe, *Undeniable*

The reasonable man adapts himself to the world: the unreasonable one persists in trying to adapt the world to himself. Therefore, all progress depends on the unreasonable man.
George Bernard Shaw, *Man and Superman*

Compact Time's Sound Base

Deep Time chronology was built on a foundation of uniformitarianism. The vast ages of the eras of the geologic column were originally derived from lengthy extrapolations of slow present-day processes. A thick cloud of doubt is gathering round the validity of this uniformitarian assumption as more and more of the column is being interpreted in terms of catastrophic events. It is now common for geoscientists to invoke impacts by asteroids, giant floods, vast volcanic lava flows, turbidity currents and other one-off high-energy events to explain geologic features. The sudden appearances of major taxa, the mass extinctions and the fossil graveyards are also hostile to uniformitarianism.

The most important backing for Deep Time was obtained from radiometric dating methods based on the radioactive decay of elements like uranium and potassium which have long half-lives. These chronometers are unsound because the two crucial assumptions underlying them can't be relied on. First, access is required to the amount of daughter element present at the time of formation of the rock unit. The popular isochron method for doing this is vulnerable. Mixing by incoming radio-elements from uprising mantle material, and/or by circulating hydrothermal fluids, leads to linear pseudo-isochrons. These are only distinguishable from genuine isochrons when the dates they produce contradict Deep Time expectations. The second assumption is that the rock unit has remained part of a closed system. Entry or exit by parent or daughter elements will invalidate use of the radiometric decay law. Rock units hundreds of millions of years old would have experienced a huge variety of intense geologic processes. Groundwaters and hydrothermal fluids continuously circulate. Magmatic intrusions heat and melt neighbouring rocks, facilitating the mobility of radio-elements. Closed-system behaviour is unlikely or non-existent. The geochronologist has to make subjective judgements about the suitability of samples based on nebulous criteria such as appearance, freshness and granularity. The failure of radiometric dating with rocks of known age throws further doubt on its validity. The default method for Deep Time is to first obtain an approximate date for materials by reference to the strata in which they appear in the geologic column. Radiometric dates at odds with this will simply be classed as outliers and discarded.

Research has shown that scientific studies are especially prone to being tainted with confirmation bias. Radiometric dating is particularly susceptible to this because of the subjective judgements and default appeals to the geologic column earth scientists habitually make. Part of the problem is that there are substantial advantages for a scientist in producing research that confirms established theories. An earth scientist's research reports will be sent for peer review to experts who are firm adherents of Deep Time. A report that supports and enlarges this view will have a better chance of publication, will be more cited and will earn the approbation of establishment scientists. The researcher's status in the field will be enhanced, and future funding assured. On the other hand, studies have shown that assessors set higher standards of evidence for hypotheses that go against their current expectations. This 'disconfirmation bias' has damaging consequences for the scientists who produce results at odds with Deep Time. The tendency of the much-vaunted peer review process is to accentuate these biases. It protects and maintains the continuity of neo-Darwinian evolution, Deep Time, and the naturalism they support. Scientists have scant motivation to seek out bias or question underlying assumptions.

Greater confidence should be placed in radiocarbon dating because it enjoys certain advantages. The half-life of ^{14}C is comparatively short, so any environmental contamination of samples decays away in a time that is brief on the conventional geologic timescale. Carbon materials tend to be held together by covalent bonds that are non-polar and so are less soluble in groundwater.[1] As a result, carbon-containing samples, such as graphite, oil, wood and bones, are far less prone to problems of contamination either by gain of incoming ^{14}C or its dissolution into circulating fluids. The radioactive metals potassium, rubidium, samarium and uranium, on the other hand, make ionic bonds in minerals and hence the resulting ions are polar and soluble in water. Rock samples are, therefore, prone to being contaminated by incoming elements and to selective loss of elements to circulating groundwater. Furthermore, because of the long half-lives, any contamination by radioactive material persists long term. These factors make radiocarbon dating inherently more reliable. There are, therefore, sound scientific reasons for distrusting Deep Time and for having confidence in radiocarbon-based Compact Time.

The finding of undecayed, residual radiocarbon throughout the geologic column is formidable evidence of a time span lasting only thousands of years. A direct consequence is that the deposition of most of the geologic column must have taken place in a recent giga-catastrophe. The reality of this is supported by the mass of folklore from every continent telling of a global flood. This event would have had a major impact on the level of radiocarbon in the biosphere. The massive burial, during the giga-catastrophe, of huge volumes of carbonaceous materials implies substantial dilution of radiocarbon before this event. Dates of specimens derived from their radiocarbon content without taking this into account would naturally be older than the true dates. Striking evidence confirming this prediction was obtained by comparing independent archaeo-historical dates for Early Bronze Age materials with their reported radiocarbon dates. Figure 5.3 affords a graphic demonstration of this.

Brown's mathematical model of the increase of ^{14}C from its dilute pre-catastrophe level to the present enables radiocarbon dates to be corrected for this. A suitable clock, appropriate for Compact Time measurements and based on analytical field data, is therefore on hand. Real Compact Time readings can easily be obtained from radiocarbon measurements and from published radiocarbon data. The CpT model dates obtained in this way matched the independent archaeo-historical dates for Bronze Age materials well. This was impressive evidence in support of the reality and timing of the giga-catastrophe.

Furthermore, the CpT model yielded dates for dinosaur fossils marginally older than five thousand years. The discoveries by Dr Mary Schweitzer and others of preserved soft tissues in dinosaur fossils are utterly incompatible with the Deep Time ages of over 66 Ma BP assigned to them. Rather, they are powerful evidence supporting the CpT dates of about five thousand years. Similar evidence of the Compact Time chronology came from the finding of preserved biological materials from specimens from throughout the geologic column. The Compact Time model was also able to resolve discordant radiocarbon dates reported for individual specimens. Overall, the Compact Time Earth chronology has many attractive features that avoid the anomalies and counter-intuitive results of Deep Time. Chart 8.1 directly compares predictions and outcomes from Deep Time (DpT) with those from Compact Time. The result is very hostile to Deep Time. Compact Time, on the other hand, leads to a coherent picture that matches archaeo-historical data. It streamlines the catastrophes of the geologic column, agrees with the short chemical lifetimes of DNA and other fossil biopolymeric materials, and tallies with folklore relating to the global flood.

The Vastness of Molecule Spaces

It's abundantly clear that Compact Time is highly inimical to neo-Darwinian evolution. It adds another voice to the growing chorus of dissent. As knowledge about the structures and properties of DNA and of proteins has grown over the last half-century, so the credibility of random, undirected neo-Darwinian

Observation/Phenomenon	Deep Time (DpT)	Compact Time (CpT)	Comment
Model and isochron ages	Based on these	Incompatible	Ages suspect; elements mobile; confirmation bias
Empty centuries	Produces them	Eliminates them	CpT remedies this anomaly for *Homo sapiens*
Persistence of fission tracks and radiohalos	Doubtful	Allows this	Delicate: vulnerable to geothermal events
Formation of Po radiohalos	Discordant	Compatible	Anomalous formation from U radiohalos in DpT
Much evidence of catastrophic geologic events	With difficulty compatible	Requires this	DpT must posit many empty gaps
Cambrian Explosion	Anomalous	Expected	DpT has no explanation; CpT envisages mass burial
Worldwide occurrence of flood folklore	Inconsistent	Predicts this	Ignored or reinterpreted by Deep Timers
Presence of ^{14}C from Cambrian to Pleistocene	Incompatible	Based on this	DpT attributes to contamination, but not in the Stone Age
^{14}C in dinosaur bones	Incompatible	Predicts this	Ignored or denied by Deep Timers
Historical dates younger than ^{14}C dates for Bronze and Stone Ages	Anomalous	Predicts this	Leads to an unresolvable impasse for Deep Timers
Soft tissues in dinosaur fossils	Incompatible	Predicts this	Deep Timers posit absurd preservation scenarios
Preserved proteins in fossils from Cambrian to Pleistocene	Incompatible	Predicts this	Ignored or denied by Deep Timers
Multitudes of polystrate trees	Incompatible	Expected	Only CpT able to explain them

Chart 8.1: *Head-to-Head Comparison of World Chronologies.*

explanations for their origin has diminished. A succession of devastating discoveries and findings have shown that this is another grand universal theory from the Victorian era that has to be given up.

The practically boundless extent of chemical space (that's the virtual domain containing all possible molecules)[2,3] is coming to the attention of more and more scientists. It's found that taking just thirty atoms and coupling them together in all possible ways can produce an enormous number of different molecules somewhere in the region of 10^{24}; that's ten followed by twenty-four zeros![4]

Pharmaceuticals typically contain many more than thirty atoms, and consequently 'drug-like' chemical space has been estimated to contain over 10^{60} molecules.[5,6] The vast size of these sets of potential molecules can be gauged by comparison with the number of stars in the known universe, which is about 10^{24}. Even these enormous molecule spaces pale into insignificance in comparison with protein or nucleic acid spaces. The number of polypeptide chains (proteins) of modest length (250 units) that could be made from the twenty natural amino acids is in excess of 10^{325}.[7] The resources of time and matter available on Earth (or in fact in the whole universe) are far too small for random, undirected searches of chemical space to find molecules with particular wanted properties.[8] Deep Time is nowhere near deep enough! Finding new antibiotics is so difficult because of the vastness of chemical space, and this is why the growing resistance of microorganisms to drugs is such a serious problem.

It is gradually being realised that no chance evolutionary process would be able to locate, amongst this almost limitless host of possible molecules, that small set of biomolecules needed to start a self-replication system, even in billions of years. Suppose some chance process existed that could examine the fitness of molecules at the fastest known speed of chemical reactions. Even this would not be able to find the molecules needed for the origin of life in four billion years. The variety of possible molecules in chemical space is just too great. It is no wonder that virtually no progress has been made in origin of life research since the famous Miller-Urey experiments in the 1950s.[9,10]

Design Eclipses Neo-Darwinian Evolution

During the last few decades, multiple problems relating to molecules-to-man evolution have come to the fore. Darwin, and his successor evolutionists, had no inkling of the astounding level of organised complexity that exists in cells. These are now known to contain many mind-blowing microscopic molecular machines such as ATP synthase that, as Figure 8.1 demonstrates, consist of ordered and matched dynamic enzyme and nucleic acid networks. These are among the most complex things in the universe. These 'irreducibly complex' systems can't be explained in terms of an evolutionary stepwise build-up of parts.[11,12]

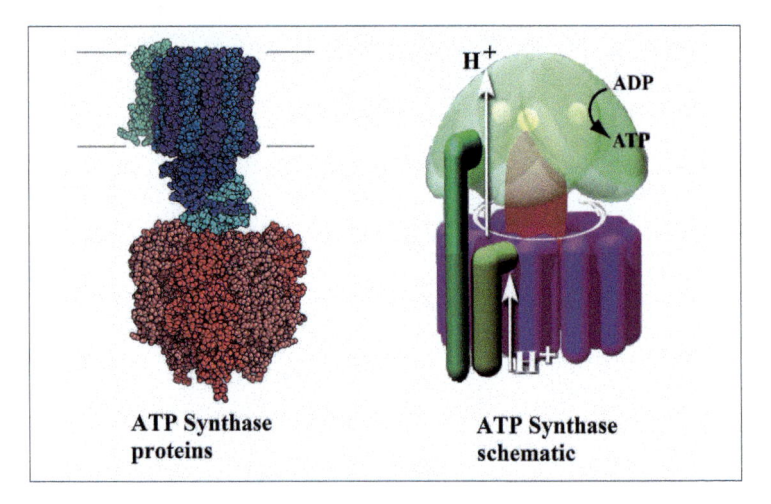

Figure 8.1: *Complex Structure of ATP Synthase Molecular Motor.*
Original photos by Alex.X and ASW-Hamburg; Wikimedia Commons CC-BY-3.0.

In living cells this genetic code is utilised by the astonishingly complex ribosome with its associated network of enzymes and nucleic acids, to make and supply the protein components as needed. Figure 8.2 sketches the outline of this.

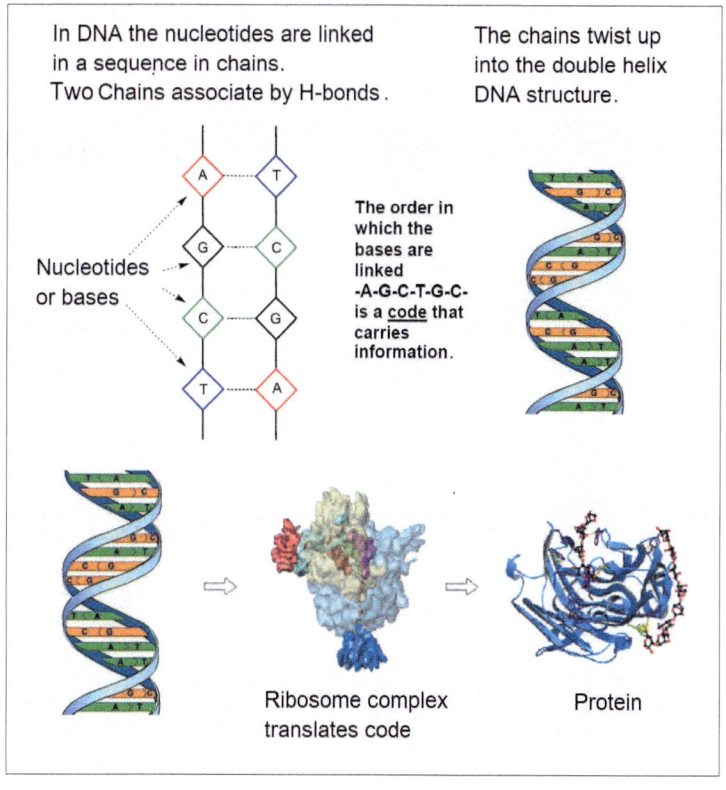

Figure 8.2: *Coded Information in the Nucleotide Sequences of DNA.*

The significance of the arrangement of the nucleotide units that make up DNA, in their double-helix structure, is also coming to light. The unique order of these nucleotide units in the DNA of each organism is a code that is passed down from generation to generation, almost without error. Where did it come from in the first place? Locating a specific nucleotide sequence in the vastness of nucleic acid space by a random search is certainly impossible.

The nucleotide order in DNA bears a strong resemblance to the order of words in a written message. The word 'order' in written texts always derives from the mind of the writer and imparts information to the reader. The nucleotide order in the DNA code carries the same sort of information. The only known sources for information of this kind are intelligent minds. The existence of these information-carrying DNA codes suggests rather persuasively that they also originated in the mind of some designer.[13,14]

Universal common descent – the assertion that all living organisms are related by common ancestry and devolve through an ancestral line – is a key evolutionary concept. Trees of life, also called phylogenetic trees, that chart hypothetical ancestry back to a single common ancestor somewhere in Deep Time, have been the backbone of evolutionary science since Darwin. Over the subsequent 150 years, many evolutionary biologists have devoted their entire lives to constructing and extending them by careful comparisons of the anatomy and morphology of living and fossil species.

Recently, however, instruments for the automatic sequencing of genes and genomes have become available and have enabled independent 'molecular trees' to be constructed. Large numbers of molecular trees, based on the sequences obtained for common genes by means of these instruments, have been put together. Far from confirming Darwin's anatomical tree, a lot of contradictory trees began to emerge as different genes from more and more species were sequenced. Some scientists began to talk about a forest of trees, while others proposed nets of relationships.[15] One scientist remarked that the tree of life was being politely buried. Biologist W. Ford Doolittle made the provocative claim that "the history of life cannot properly be represented as a tree".[16] Only tangled webs of relationships remained! The foundation on which the concept of common ancestry rested has crumbled away. By carefully selecting data they consider relevant, some scientists continue to trace a 'tree signal' in these forests of relationships. The subjectivity of this is obvious, as is the likelihood of intervention from confirmation bias and experimenter expectancy!

The mutation/random selection mechanism by which neo-Darwinian evolution proceeds has also come under fire. New structural themes in living organisms manifest themselves in new protein folds. Douglas Axe and others made biochemical tests of the effect of mutations on protein folds and concluded that functional changes could not emerge by neo-Darwinian means even in billions of years.[17,18] Other scientists who have investigated protein and nucleic acid responses to mutations with selection have also concluded that this mechanism does not possess the creative power to produce genuine biological innovation.[19,20] It's not surprising, therefore, that the famous laboratory experiments of T. H. Morgan, E. Mayr and many others, inducing mutations in fruit flies, *E. coli* and other organisms over many generations, revealed only degenerative changes.

The story of junk DNA being dead genes (the vestigial remnants of evolution), touted in many biology textbooks as convincing proof of neo-Darwinism,[21] has also completely unravelled thanks to the ENCODE project.[22] Of course, there is plenty of evidence for the special theory of evolution, also called microevolution. These comparatively small changes and adaptations take place rapidly and pose no problem for Compact Time.

Compact Time and Belief Systems

Compact Time provides a chronological framework for belief systems about the origin and development of living organisms on Earth. It is not unscientific, because it stems from a novel understanding of radiocarbon dating. Neither is it at war with science as such, but only with uniformitarian earth science and neo-Darwinian historical biology. Compact Time banishes hundreds of millions of years from the geologic column. It joins the discoveries outlined above and amplifies their evidence controverting neo-Darwinism. Without Deep Time there is no temporal window in which neo-Darwinian evolution could possibly operate. Thankfully, the evolutionists' concept of human beings as fragile DNA capsules struggling to avoid extinction in predator-infested biological broth is revealed as no more than a nightmarish fantasy.

Compact Time radically alters humanity's status in the world. No longer need human life be viewed as a tiny interlude, a brief flowering of biological complexity, lost in fourteen billion years of random interactions of matter and energy in an indifferent universe. Rather, one human lifespan makes a small but significant contribution when compared with a total earth history lasting only thousands of years. Mankind, together with all the plant and animal kingdoms, came into existence in a short space of time. Consequently, man's ancestry owes nothing to apes, nor to any other living species. He has not inherited animal instincts. Human intellect is profoundly superior to all animal kinds. All known languages are multifaceted and are supplemented by complex systems of communication. Human beings are distinct from all animals in their use of abstract thought and mental symbols to reflect on intangible things. The idea of living by fierce competition for resources, for habitats, and to promote evolutionary progress can be cheerfully dismissed!

Naturalism, the belief that nature contains all of reality – or, as Carl Sagan pithily put it, "The Cosmos is all that is or ever was or ever will be"[23] – has long relied on neo-Darwinian evolution as one of its principal scientific credentials. With the removal of this prop, naturalism's claims appear threadbare. One can legitimately join the flight from this chill realm, from the pitiless indifference of its cosmos, from its angry prophets, and from the individual and corporate extinction so bravely embraced by its citizens. It is undoubtedly time to think outside the physico-temporal constraints of naturalism's ideological box.

Several belief systems, mainly Christian, cluster under the heading of 'theistic evolution' or 'evolutionary creation'. Some of these religions advocate the creative power of the neo-Darwinian mechanism of mutation and natural selection. Others maintain the idea that all organisms are related by common descent. They attempt by various expedients to harmonise these evolutionary ideas with the creative activity of God.[24] These religions envisage wasteful and supremely slow gods. They, with their troubling and inefficient deities, are incompatible with Compact Time chronology and can also be laid aside.

Remarkably, the distinctive features of Compact Time are commensurate with the origins account as it appears in Genesis. The time period from the present to the giga-catastrophe roughly corresponds to that deduced from the genealogies in Genesis. The giga-catastrophe and the global flood described in Genesis are essentially the same. Both last a comparatively short time, both result in the rapid deposition of sedimentary and igneous strata, and both bring about the prompt burial and fossilisation of all land organisms. Both explain the sudden appearance of species, their biological stasis, and the mass extinctions. Both lead to the expectation of finding soft tissues in dinosaur and other fossils. Both posit that living organisms, including human beings, owe their existence to a Designer/Creator. Genesis is clearly describing the same global event.

In the context of astrophysical discoveries, Robert Jastrow aptly wrote, in *God and the Astronomers*:

> *For the scientist who has lived by his faith in the power of reason, the story ends like a bad dream. He has scaled the mountain of ignorance, he is about to conquer the highest peak; as he pulls himself over the final rock, he is greeted by a band of theologians who have been sitting there for centuries.*[25]

It seems the same bad dream awaits evolutionary scientists. Those who follow the evidence and struggle free of naturalism's straitjacket find themselves greeted by a small band of Old Testament theologians! Admittedly, it will be a small band containing only those of conservative persuasion.

Both Genesis and the Compact Time scenario envisage all living creatures coming into existence in a well-designed environment in a short space of time. Because proceedings were so coordinated, the start-up of nature's many complex cycles is rendered intelligible. The rapid and coordinated beginning accords well with the networks of interrelationships and interdependencies observed everywhere in nature amongst diverse species. That the environment on Earth is amazingly well designed is steadily being realised. Now that over five thousand exoplanets have been discovered, the perception of Earth as average or insignificant has dramatically declined. Nowhere else yet discovered has anything approaching Earth's mix of special circumstances ideally suited to the support of life.

The evidence that life on Earth originated with a Designer/Creator is mounting up. The pile has reached such proportions that denying or ignoring it is becoming irrational. It's time to move out of the shadow of naturalism and to ask questions about who this Designer/Creator is, what is his nature and what are his intentions towards humankind.[26] What could be the nature of a being with attributes far exceeding those of humans; attributes sufficient to bring about such a huge and complex task? Is he still involved with the material universe, and if so, how? Is he a personal or impersonal being? Does he communicate with humanity, and if so, how? Why is he so elusive of scientific discovery? Answers to these questions are hugely important for the individual. Everything of material, ethical and moral importance depends on them. No avenues, whether scientific, spiritual or inspirational, should be neglected in seeking answers. The Compact Time chronology for earth history is another of the discoveries tending to authenticate the historicity of the Hebrew scriptural narratives. These scriptures have emerged largely unscathed from the intense critical attacks of the last century.[27] The remarkably accurate historical, cultural and geographical information they contain bears out this dependability. Genesis seems an excellent place to start searching for answers.[28]

Chapter 8: References and Notes

1. The exceptions to this, of course, are the oxides, carbonate and bicarbonate, which are ionic and so soluble in water.
2. J-L. Reymond, 'The chemical space project' in *Accounts of Chemical Research*, 2015, *48*, pp. 722–30.
3. R. S. Bon and H. Waldmann, 'Bioactivity-guided navigation of chemical space' in *Accounts of Chemical Research*, 2010, *43*, pp. 1,103–14.
4. P. Ertl, 'Cheminformatics analysis of organic substituents: identification of the most common substituents, calculation of substituent properties, and automatic identification of drug-like bioisosteric groups' in *Journal of Chemical Information and Computer Sciences*, 2003, *43*, pp. 374–80.
5. C. A. Lipinski, F. Lombardo, B. W. Dominy and P. J. Feeney, 'Experimental and computational approaches to estimate solubility and permeability in drug discovery and development settings' in *Advanced Drug Delivery Reviews*, 1997, *23*, pp. 3–25.
6. R. S. Bohacek, C. McMartin and W. C. Guida, 'The art and practice of structure-based drug design: a molecular modeling perspective' in *Medicinal Research Reviews*, 1996, *16*, pp. 3–50.
7. M. Eigen, 'Self-organization of matter and the evolution of biological macromolecules' in *Naturwissenschaften*, 1971, *58*, pp. 465–523.
8. P. Ball, 'Navigating chemical space' in *Chemistry World*, October 2015, pp. 58–61.
9. J. Tour, in *Theistic Evolution*, J. P. Moreland, S. C. Meyer, C. Shaw, A. K. Gauger and W. Grudem (eds.), Crossway, Wheaton, Illinois, 2017, pp. 165–91.
10. J. C. Walton, 'The origin of life: scientists play dice' in *Should Christians Embrace Evolution?*, N. C. Nevin (ed.), IVP, Nottingham, 2009, Ch. 11, pp. 187–209.
11. (a) M. J. Behe, *Darwin Devolves*, HarperOne, New York, 2019; (b) M. J. Behe, *Darwin's Black Box*, second edition, Free Press, 2006.
12. M. Eberlin, *Foresight*, Discovery Institute Press, Seattle, 2019.
13. (a) S. C. Meyer, *Darwin's Doubt*, HarperOne, New York, 2013; (b) S. C. Meyer, *Signature in the Cell*, HarperOne, New York, 2009.

14. J. C. Walton, 'Organization and the Origin of Life' in *Origins*, 1977, *4*, pp 16-35
15. G. Lawton, 'Why Darwin was wrong about the tree of life' in *New Scientist*, 21st January 2009.
16. W. F. Doolittle, 'Phylogenetic classification and the universal tree' in *Science*, 1999, *284*, pp. 2,124-8.
17. (a) D. D. Axe, 'Estimating the prevalence of protein sequences adopting functional enzyme folds' in *Journal of Molecular Biology*, 2004, *341*, pp. 1,295-315; (b) A. K. Gauger and D. D. Axe, 'The evolutionary accessibility of new enzyme functions: a case study from the biotin pathway' in *BIO-Complexity*, 2011, *1*, pp. 1-17.
18. D. D. Axe, *Undeniable*, HarperCollins, 2016, Ch. 6, pp. 81-6.
19. M. Leisola, in *Theistic Evolution*, J. P. Moreland, S. C. Meyer, C. Shaw, A. K. Gauger and W. Grudem (eds.), Crossway, Wheaton, Illinois, 2017, Ch. 3, pp. 139-63.
20. For a very accessible account of this see D. Williams, *Taken Without Consent*, Kindle Direct Publishing, 2020.
21. See for example J. Coyne, *Why Evolution is True*, Oxford University Press, 2009, p. 71.
22. M. B. Gerstein, A. Kundaje, M. Hariharan, S. G. Landt, K-K. Yan, C. Cheng, X. J. Mu, E. Khurana, J. Rozowsky, R. Alexander et al., 'Architecture of the human regulatory network derived from ENCODE data' in *Nature*, 2012, *489*, pp. 91-100.
23. C. Sagan, *Cosmos*, Abacus, London, 2003.
24. For a comprehensive critique of theistic evolution see *Theistic Evolution*, J. P. Moreland, S. C. Meyer, C. Shaw, A. K. Gauger and W. Grudem (eds.), Crossway, Wheaton, Illinois, 2017.
25. R. Jastrow, *God and the Astronomers*, Norton, 1978.
26. For an in dept philosophical treatment of the existence of God and his attributes see: E. Feser, *Five Proofs of the Existence of God*' Ignatius Press, San Francisco, 2017.
27. See for example (a) D. Graves, *The Archaeology of the Old Testament: 115 Discoveries That Support the Reliability of the Bible*, independently published, ISBN-10: 1692356100, 2019; (b) C. L. Blomberg, *The Historical Reliability of the New Testament*, B&H Academic, Nashville, 2016; (c) C. Anderson and B. Edwards, *Evidence for the Bible*, Day One, Leominster, 2014; (d) P. R. Eddy and G. A. Boyd, *The Jesus Legend: A Case*

for the Historical Reliability of the Synoptic Jesus Tradition, Baker Publishing, Grand Rapids, 2007; (e) D. N. Marshall, *The Battle for the Bible*, Autumn House, Grantham, 2004; (f) K. A. Kitchen, *On the Reliability of the Old Testament*, Eerdmans, Cambridge, UK, 2003.

28. For answers try (a) J. W. Wallace, *God's Crime Scene: A Cold-Case Detective Examines the Evidence for a Divinely Created Universe*, David C. Cook, Colorado Springs, 2015; (b) J. C. Lennox, *God's Undertaker: Has Science Buried God?*, Lion, Oxford, 2007; (c) W. L. Craig, *Reasonable Faith*, third edition, Crossway, Wheaton, 2008; (d) N. T. Wright, *The Resurrection of the Son of God*, second edition, SPCK Publishing, 2017; (e) L. Strobel, *The Case for Faith*, Zondervan, 2014; (f) C. S. Lewis, *Mere Christianity*, Collins, 2012.

General Index

abiogenesis, 138
academic elite, 52
accelerator mass spectrometry, (AMS) 37, 40, 42, 44, 79, 90, 95, 136
actinium, 9
actualism, 53
age of the earth, 3, 6, 13, 136
Ager, Derek, 56, 57, 103
alpha decay process, 21
amber, 110
amino acid dating, 80
amino acids, 105, 114, 147
ammonites, 113
anatomical tree, 150
ancestral tales, 72
ancient carbon, 39
ancient coal, 39, 40, 42
ancient DNA, 107, 110
Angiosperm Big Bloom, 130
animal instincts, 152
antioxidant, 105
antique objects, 39
apocalyptic event, 72
apparent isochron, 18
archaeo-historical, 85, 90, 91, 94, 95, 145

archaeo-historical chronology, 91
archaeo-historical dates, 85, 90
argon, 14, 19, 28
Armitage, Mark, xvii, 46, 47, 108
arrow of time, 2
Aryan mythology, 6
Ashkelon, 91
asteroid impacts, 55
Aston, Francis, 7
atmospheric CO_2 level, 33, 96
atomic bomb testing, 81
ATP synthase, 148
Atrahasis epic, 68
Aurignacian, 118, 119
Australopithecines, 135
Australopithecus Afarensis, 28
authentication of antiques, 39
automatic sequencing, 150
Axe, Douglas, 141, 151
Aztec, 69

Bacon, Francis, 1
Baillie, M. G. L., 99
Behrensmeyer, Kay, 26
belief systems, xviii, 151, 153
bell-shaped distribution, 95
Beta-counting devices, 37

♦ 159

biofilm, 106
biological markers, 138
biological stasis, 153
biomolecules, 105, 112, 147
biopolymers, 105, 121
biotite, 21
Bishop, Bill, 26
Blue Mountains, 131
boat or ark, 67, 69, 92
bogs, 80, 97
Bohunician, 118, 120
bone collagen, 116
bone flutes, 118
Bragg, W. Lawrence, vi
Braun, E., 87
bristlecone pines, 74, 75, 94, 95, 97
Brock, Andrew, 27, 28
Brongniart, Adolphe-Théodore, 4
Bronze Age, 38, 86, 88, 90
Brown, Robert H., 80, 81, 82, 90, 116
Bruins, H. J., 86, 90
Buffon, George-Louis, 13
Bulawayan group, 137
Burgess Shale, 56, 115

calibrated ^{14}C ages, 84, 85, 88, 92, 93, 104, 136
calibration methods, 90
Cambrian, 9, 13, 22, 41, 61, 128, 130, 136, 137, 146
Cambrian Explosion, 130, 138, 146
carbon dioxide, 2, 35, 36, 105, 114
carbonate rocks, 73, 111
Carboniferous, 130
carboxylic acids, 105
Carlsbad, 114
cave art, 119

cave deposits, 80
Cenozoic, 5, 42, 43, 47, 127
chain reaction, 59, 61, 109
Chalcolithic, 93
Channelled Scablands, 54
Châtelperronian culture, 118, 120
Chauvet cave, 118
Chekurovka mammoth, 116
chemical fossils, 138
chemical space, 147, 148
chemical stabilizers, 105
Chicxulub, 55
Chinese culture, 67
Chitin, 115
Christian Malford, 113
Clarey, T., 63
clay catalysts, 105
clay minerals, 137
clonal plants, 73
closed system, 9, 73, 142
coal, 34, 39, 42, 43, 73, 95, 111, 131
Cody, George, 114
coelacanths, 131
coleoid, 113
collagen, 45, 109, 116
collagen degradation, 109
common ancestry, 150, 151
common descent, 150, 153
Compact Time chronology, 121, 127, 130, 145, 153, 155
confirmation bias, 1, 10, 24, 26, 29, 30, 143, 146, 151
Confucius, 66
Cooke, Basil, 27, 28
co-regencies, 89
cosmic rays, 35
counting equipment, 90
Cow Branch Formation, 56

Coxcox, 69
Coyne, Jerry, xiv, xxi
CpT dates, 108, 111, 145
Cremo, M. A., 135
Cretaceous, 4, 46, 54, 55, 112, 130
Crichton, Michael, 78
Cro-Magnon, 118
crustaceans, 113
cultural mindset, xv, 51
cuneiform tablet, 68
Curie, Marie, 7
Curtis, Garniss, 27, 28, 29

Darwin, Charles, xix, 13, 129, 148, 150
Darwin, Erasmus, 13
daughter elements, 11, 14, 48, 142
Dead Sea Scrolls, 39
Debs, Eugene V., 103
Deccan Traps, 55
default mode, 23, 133
dendrochronology, 89, 94, 98, 99
Deucalion and Pyrrha, 67
DeYoung, Don, 42
Diderot, Denis, 13
dinosaur fossils, 46, 95, 103–107, 110, 121, 145, 146
dinosaurs, 44, 46, 55, 104, 130
dipole strength, 80
discordant isochron, 20
DNA in Egyptian mummies, 109
DNA sequencing, 118
Doolittle, W. F., 150
double-blind experiments, 26
double-helix, 149

Early Bronze Age, 86, 87, 91, 121, 144

earth's magnetic field, 80
E-coli, 151
Eddington, Arthur, 2
Ediacaran, 137
Edwards, N. P., 111
Egypt, 67, 85, 87, 93
Egyptian archaeological sites, 109
Egyptian chronologies, 86
Egyptian mummies, 109, 110
Egyptian Old Kingdom, 87
Eldredge, Niles, 129
Emiran stone tools, 118, 120
empty centuries, 88, 119, 121, 146
ENCODE project, 151
Enki, 68
Enlil, 68
entropy, 2
ER 1470 skull, 27, 28
erratic dates, 118
eurypterid, 115
evolutionary creation, 153
excess argon, 19
exoplanets, 154
experimenter bias, 25
experimenter expectancy, 24, 151
extinct apes, 135
extrusive igneous activity, 62

Fairbanks Creek, 116
Ferguson Farm mastodon, 116
Feynman, Richard P., 51, 103, 127
Fig Tree group, 137
figurines, 118, 119
first intermediate period, 108
fission track dating, 27, 29
flood basalts, 55, 62, 63
flood legends, narratives & stories, 66–75

folklore, 66, 71, 72, 144, 145, 146
fossil dinosaur tissues, 110
fossil footprints, 135
fossil graveyards, 56, 58, 62, 142
fossil hominid bones, 26
fossil ink, 113
fossil squid, 113
Francis Creek shale, 56
free radicals, xviii
Frost, Robert, 78
fruit flies, 151
fungal colonies, 73

garnets, 19, 20
Geiger counters, 34, 37
genealogies in Genesis, 153
Genesis, xix, 67–72, 153–155
Genesis account of Noah, 70
Genesis flood narrative, 67
genetic code, 149
geological timescale, 11, 12, 58
geologically closed system, 9
German oaks, 94
Giem, Paul, 40, 111
Gilgamesh epic, 68
Gleadow, Andrew, 27–29
global catastrophe, 3, 80, 84, 89
global flood, 70–75, 144, 145, 153
glycoproteins, 114
Gould, Stephen J., 130
Grand Banks, 53
Grand Canyon, 16, 20, 60, 116
granite batholiths, 7
graphite, 40, 44, 136, 143
graphitic materials, 138
Gravettian, 118–120
Great Isaiah Scroll, 39

Green River Formation, 111
ground sloths, 116
growth rings, 73

Haas, H., 87
haemoglobin, 40, 111
Haldane, J. B. S., 136
half-life, 11, 19, 20, 35, 37–42, 48, 81, 109, 136, 143
Hamelin Pool, 137
Hasel, Michael G., 86
Hell Creek Formation, 46, 47, 106
historical chronologies, 85
Holmes, Arthur, 6–14
homo sapiens, xix, 118–121, 146, 135–156
Honshu, 58
horseshoe crab, 130
Hurford, Anthony, 27, 28, 29
Hutton, James, 3
Huxley, Thomas H., 13
hydrolytic degradation, 132
hydrothermal fluids, 10, 23, 142

ice age, 62, 127
igneous formations, 103
igneous provinces, 62
igneous strata, 153
immunoglobulins, 114
ink sac, 113
IntCal13 calibration curve, 94–96, 136
intermediate organisms, 138
intrusive, 62, 63, 133–136
investigator predisposition, 19
Irish oaks, 94
iron particles, 110
irreducibly complex, 148

Isaac, Glynn, 27, 28
isochron age, 15, 18
isochron method, 14, 16, 17, 19, 142
Isua Greenstone, 138
ivory, 39, 116, 118, 119

Jastrow, Robert, 153
Jeans, James, 33
Jericho, 86, 87, 91, 119
Joggins Formation, 131
Johanson, Don, 28
Joly, John, 5
Junk DNA, 151
Jurassic Oxford clay, 113
Jurassic Period, 4, 46, 131

Kanapoi, 135
K-Ar method, 17, 27
KBS Tuff, 17, 26, 27
kerogen, 138
Kishenehn Formation, 111
Knapp, Arthur, 87
Koobi Fora, 26, 27
K/T extinction, 55

Lac Courte Oreilles Ojibwa, 67
Laetoli, 135
Lake Missoula, xvi
Lake Turkana, 26, 28
Lamarck, Jean-Baptiste, 13
Lazarus bacteria, 114
lead isotopes, 8, 9
lead migration, 19
lead ores, 9
Leakey family, 26
Leakey, Louis, 28, 134
Leakey, Mary, 135
Leakey, Richard, 26, 27, 29

Libby half-life, 38
Libby, Willard, 34–38
Lindgren, J., 112
living fossils, 131
Llangernyw Yew, 73
log mat, 61
Lord Vishnu, 68
Lucy, 28
Lyell, Sir Charles, 4

Magdalenian, 118–120
magmatic rocks, 53, 63, 142
Malthus, T. R., 13
Mammalian Radiation, 130
mammoths, 116
mantle, 10, 18, 19, 23, 44, 58, 142
mantle inheritance, 13, 19
mantle isochrons, 18
Manu, 68
Marine13, 94, 95
mass extinctions, 53, 55, 103, 130, 142, 153
mass spectrometry, 7, 37
master chronology, 98, 99
Matsya, 68
Mayr, Ernst, 130, 151
Mazar, Amihai, 87
McDougall, Ian, 28, 29
mean radiocarbon life, 81
melanin, 114
Mellaart, James, 86, 91
Mesopotamia, 68, 71, 85
Mesozoic, 42, 43, 127
methodological naturalism, 30
methodological rigour, xvii
Methuselah, 74
microbial communities, 137
microevolution, 132, 151

microfossils, 137, 138
Middle Eastern, 38, 91
Middle Eocene, 111
Middle Palaeolithic, 41, 42
Miller, Hugh, 47
Miller, Jack, 26, 27, 28
Miller-Urey experiment, 148
mineral isochron age, 15
Minoan Santorini eruption, 91
mixing isochron, 18
moa bird, 109
model ages, 14, 17, 84, 85, 93, 105
modern skeleton, 113
molecular machines, 148
molecular tree, 150
molecule space, 145, 147
Montceau Basin, 56
Montmorillonite, 139
Morgan, T. H., 151
mosasaur, 112
mosquito, 111
Mount St. Helens, xvi, 59–62
mountains of Ararat, 69
Mousterian, 41, 118, 120
Mt. Ngauruhoe, 16, 17
mudslides, 53
Munich, 134
Murchison, Sir Roderick, 4
musk ox, 116
myth, xix, 71

Natufian, 119, 120
naturalism, xv, xvii, xix, 30, 51, 143, 152, 154
Nautilus, 130
Neanderthals, 118
Near Eastern civilizations, 89

neo-Darwinian evolution, xv–xx, 136, 143, 145, 148–153
neodymium, 14, 15, 19, 20
neutron flux, 40
neutrons, 34, 35, 40
Nim Chimpsky, 25
Noah, 69, 70
nuclear tests, 37, 41
nucleic acid network, 148
nucleic acid space, 147
nucleotide, 149, 150

ocean warming, 62
oceanic crust, 62
Old Testament, 154
old wood problem, 88
Olduvai Gorge, 133, 134
Onverwacht group, 137
open system, 16, 17, 19, 20
oral traditions, 67, 70
organelle-like structures, 106
origin of human life, 133
origin of life, 148
out of Africa, 133
outliers, 24, 116, 142
oxidation, 104, 105
oxidative degradation, 105, 132

Pacific mammoth, 116
Palaeolithic, 41, 118, 120, 127
Palaeolithic cultures, 120, 121
Palaeolithic sites, 41, 42
Paleochronology Group, 45, 47
paleomagnetic data, 80
paleomagnetic reversals, 27
Paleozoic, 5, 42, 43, 127
Palestine, 91
Palestinian archaeology, 87

palladium-119, 22
panspermia, 139
Parana Plateau, 55
Parkes, John, 114
particulates, 62
PCR method, 109
peer review, 143
Pennsylvanian, 115
Pentateuch, 6
peptide sequences, 106
Permian, 43, 55, 114
photosynthesis, 33, 35
phylogenetic tree, 150
phytane, 138
Piltdown affair, 25
Pitchblende, 7, 9
Plato, 67
pleochroic halos, 21
Plous, Scott, 1
polonium, 7, 21, 22
polonium radiohalos, 21, 22
polymerase chain reaction (PCR), 109
polypeptide chains, 147
polystrate trees, xvi, 62, 131, 146
porphyrins, 111, 138
potassium-argon, 14, 19, 20, 135
Precambrian atmosphere, 136
Precambrian fossils, 137
pre-catastrophic atmosphere, 80
Predynastic period, 87, 93
pre-Pleistocene, 40, 42, 95, 135
preservative reagents, 105
preserving proteins, 110
primate fossils, 133
primates, 132
primordial soup, 136, 138
pristane, 138

Prometheus, 67
Prose Edda, 67
protein folds, 151
protein segments, 108
protons, 34
Protsch, Reiner, 134
pseudo-isochrons, 18, 19, 142
public conditioning, 52
punctuated equilibrium, 130

Quaternary, 38

radioactive decay law, 11, 36
radiohalos, 22, 146
radioisotope techniques, 80
radiometric age, 23, 73
radiometric dating, xvi–xx, 6, 10, 14, 15, 16, 20, 26, 109, 118, 120, 142, 143
radium, 7, 8
Rampart Cave, 116
Raup, David M., 129
Rb-Sr isochron, 18, 19
Reck, Hans, 133, 134
reflection pulse, 59, 61
Regev, J., 91
reinterpretation, 133, 134
repair mechanisms, 105
reptiles, 108
Revised chronologies, 88
ribosomal DNA, 114
ribosome, 149
Rig-Vedas, 6
ring count, 73, 74
ring widths, 96
RNA world, 139
Rohl, David M., 86–88, 91
Roosevelt, Theodore, 66

rubidium, 15, 143, 148
rubidium-strontium, 20
Rupe, C., 135

Sagan, C., 152
Salado salt formation, 114
salt in the sea, 6
samarium, 15, 48, 143
samarium-neodymium, 14, 19, 20
Sanford, J. C., 135
Santana Formation, 56
Schoch, Robert, 69
Schopenhauer, Arthur, 33
Schweitzer, Mary H., xvii, 106, 107, 110, 145
sea scorpion, 115
sea urchins, 130
second law of thermodynamics, 2
Sedgwick, Adam, 4
sedimentary hourglasses, 6
sedimentary strata, 4, 5, 53
self-replication, 147
Sendai, 58, 59
sequencing, 5, 109, 110, 150
Sequoia National Park, 73
seven sages, 68
Shark Bay, 137
Shaw, George B., 141
Siberian Platform, 55
signing apes, 25
Silurian, 115
sister isotope, 15
Smith, William, 4
Snelling, Andrew, xi, 18, 20, 53, 57
Snorri Sturluson, 67
sodium, 5
soft dinosaur tissues, 106, 108

soft tissues, xvii, 44, 46, 103–115, 121, 145, 146, 153
Solutrean, 118–120
sphere of discolouration, 21
Spirit Lake, 60, 61
sponges, 115
springs of the great deep, 69
stable carbon isotopes, 138
Stone Age civilizations, 118
Stone Age epochs, 119, 120
stone tools, 118, 119
Storegga suite, 54
stratosphere, 61, 62
stromatolites, 137
strontium, 15, 20
Sumer, 68
sun's photosphere, 80
sunspot activity, 80
symbiotic relationship, 94
Szent-Györgi, Albert, 51

tectonic movement, 59
Tell el-Dabᶜa, 91
Tell el-Umeiri, 91
Tepexi Limestone, 56
Terrace, Herbert, 25
Tertiary strata, 9, 41, 42
Tezpi, 69
theistic evolution, 153
Thompson, R. L., 135
Thorite, 9
thorium, 7–9, 14, 19, 21
Thunder Bay Limestone, 56
Tiktaalik, xiv
Tohoku, 58–61
Toltec story, 69
Torbernite, 7
Toutle river, 60

transitional species, 130
tree of life, 150
tree ring chronology, 99
tree ring dating, 94
Tree ring patterns, 96
tree ring width variations, 94
tree signal, 151
triceratops, xvii, 45–47, 104, 108
trilobites, 55, 130
tsunami, 9, 58, 59, 61, 63, 72
t-test values, 98
turbidites, xvi, 54, 58
turbidity currents, 53, 143
Turin Shroud, 39
Tutankhamun, 109
Tyrannosaurus, 106
tyrosinase, 114

Uinkaret plateau, 16, 17
ultra-high chronologies, 88
uncalibrated radiocarbon ages, 84, 85
unconscious bias, xvii, 10, 24
uniformitarian, 3, 5, 52, 89, 141, 152
uniformitarianism, 3, 4, 53, 141, 142
Upper Palaeolithic, 118, 120
Uraninite, 9
uranium, 7–9, 19–22, 34, 37, 48, 142, 144

uranium radiohalos, 21, 22
Urry, W. D., 8
Utnapishtim, 68

van der Plicht, J., 86, 90
Vendian, 137
Venus figurines, 118, 119
vestigial genes, 151
Vinland Map, 39
Vreeland, Russell, 114

Wallace, Alfred R., 13
Washoe, 25
White, Tim, 28
whole rock isochron age, 15, 16
width patterns, 98
wiggles, 90, 94, 95
Wilby, Philip, 113, 114
Wollemi pine, 131

Xia and Zhou dynasties, 67

Yarmuth, 91
Yucatan peninsula, 55

Zeus, 67
zircon, 21
Ziusudra, 68

ABOUT THE AUTHOR

John Walton was born into the rationing, air raids and turmoil of World War 2. He had a traditional Grammar School education in England and learned to love science. He studied chemistry at Sheffield University before moving to Scotland to start his academic career at the University of Dundee. Soon afterwards Lord Tedder invited him to join the School of Chemistry at St. Andrews University, where he eventually became Research Professor of Chemistry. He loves research and embarking on adventures of the mind. He is recognized as a world expert on free radicals and never tires of observing their entropic dances in chemical space. He has written hundreds of specialized papers as well as two books on Free Radical Chemistry. He has been visiting professor at several universities in Europe as well as an invited guest on many occasions at the National Research Council of Canada. He has a lively interest in matters relating to science and faith and has written and lectured on this theme in the UK and overseas. He lives with his bonny wife in picturesque St. Andrews beside the grey-green sea.

Matador

For exclusive discounts on Matador titles,
sign up to our occasional newsletter at
troubador.co.uk/bookshop